Bones & Jokes

Bones & Jokes

Ted Jonathan

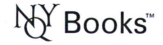

The New York Quarterly Foundation, Inc.
New York, New York

NYQ Books™ is an imprint of The New York Quarterly Foundation, Inc.

The New York Quarterly Foundation, Inc.
P. O. Box 2015
Old Chelsea Station
New York, NY 10113

www.nyqbooks.org

First Edition

Set in Georgia typeface.

Layout and Design by Raymond P. Hammond
Cover Art and Photo by Brooke Larsen

Library of Congress Control Number: 2009929140

ISBN: 978-1-935520-01-6

In memory of my mother,
Ann Greenberg
(1930-1968)

Also by Ted Jonathan

Spiked Libido (1998)

Acknowledgments

Special thanks to the editors of journals where these poems and stories, some in earlier versions, first appeared: "These Words Are of No Help to Holly," "Son of Sam," "Regina Einhorn," "what goes down must come up," "Tommy Bolan," "Damon's Way," "Hurly-Burly Buroo," "The President's Daughter Caught a Big Fish in Kennebunkport," "Straight Lines," "A Better Man," "Third Floor," "Salamanders," "Redemption," *The New York Quarterly*; "Haircut," "Chinatown," "White Men in Sandals," "God's Honey," "The Essential Dentistry of Dr. Jack Kreeger," "Uptown Express," "Ballad of Caleb Belleu," "The Healing," *Skidrow Penthouse*; "A Lion is a Cow," "Simeon," "One Day in November," "On Maxie Off," "Kiss of Death," *Iconoclast*; "A Jewish Giant at Home with his Parents in the Bronx, N.Y. 1970," *Slant*; "Letter to Lori Waterhouse," *The Hiram Poetry Review*; "To the Light, Darkly," *Dirty Napkin*; "From the Diary of a Prizefighter," *Web Del Sol Review*; "Grace," *Jewish Currents*; "the sweetest dream," "The Volunteer," *Main Street Rag;* "Jay Spenser," *Fight These Bastards*.

My gratitude to those who helped with these poems and stories: Robert E. Mills, Tony Gloeggler, and Sophia Howes. And to my friend and mentor, the late great William Packard.

Table of Contents

POEMS

STORIES

Poems

These Words Are of No Help to Holly

At 51, Holly is the oldest resident at the Bronx
homeless shelter for women. Her barn owl face—features
large circular glasses in a brown plastic frame, resting
—low—on the bridge of her nose. Flabby but healthy—
with grayish-brown hair—she is the only white resident.

Tomorrow will be Christmas. Her first in 12 years without
Pumpkin and Rhett—her two mixed-breed dogs. She used to
celebrate Christmas with them, in her tiny Washington
Heights apartment that the three of them shared.
At the foot of the small fresh tree would be three care-
fully wrapped gifts. Every year, the dogs would knock
the tree down, and Holly'd go through the motions of
scolding them—inwardly, delighting in their traditional
mischief.

Within the past year both dogs died. Alone—she'd sleep
most all the time. The temp-agency stopped calling altogether.
She lost her tiny apartment. Under her bed at the shelter
—and always—within arms reach, is a 4 ounce Maxwell House
instant coffee jar. The red plastic lid—of which—has
been twisted shut tight. It contains the ashes of her dogs.
It is a small glass jar—with a red label.

Son of Sam

Clapping, he'd look around; at the other boys on
his side of the volleyball court who were clapping.
When they stopped, he stopped.

Burly, friendless, and blank—

Berkowitz. In black dress socks, gym shorts, and
sneakers. Back in high school gym class.

Spent a couple years as a peacetime soldier, and moved
on to become a nighttime postal worker; before he got
busted for being—

Son of Sam. Girl hunter who'd thunder them bloody with
his 44. A self-described, "chubby behemoth." Who heard
his killing orders in the—

Barking. Out his window. In the alley. Sam Carr's dog—
BARKING BARKING BARKING BARKING—

Berkowitz. Showed you. Chose to. Show you.
KILLING KILLING KILLING KILLING—

BREATH-ING!

Regina Einhorn

(written after my cancer diagnosis, 11/2/06)

What planet she's
dropped from,
nobody knows.

She hunts alone.

Coolly cruising
Rochambeau Avenue:
legs and
more legs, casual hips,
jagged shag, pillow lips,
and a mannish
two finger pinch
on her Parliament.

17, and
she out-Klutes
Jane Fonda.

A mixed pack
of cocksure
Bib & Sam's candy
store hanging deep-
toking James Dean-
afflicted egomaniacs
flex their blue jean
buttocks, but she
somehow plucks me.

Makes a man feel—
so proud.

Chats Fender
Stratocaster and
Gibson SG.
Tells me to read
Narcissus and Goldmund.
And that she's tight with
Humble Pie.

Seeks:
"A real good-looking
guy with sensitive eyes,
to hang with locally."

Last night I was too
stoned to crawl out
of a two-feet-deep
Bronx Park East ditch.

Tonight,
amid the brush, beneath
the silver carving moon,
it's me and blue-denim
miniskirt clad, red
lipstick adorned, rooted
Regina.

"I feel *very* submissive,"
she says, nonchalantly.

"Hummana, hummana, hummana..."
I am Ralph Kramden.
And hear the soft, low,
surging trill of a small
(voyeuristic?) owl, before
I collapse inwardly.

*****

Across a great green lawn,
hand in hand, walks Regina,
with another man.

And I wonder,
where in this melted pot
Bronx Gehenna did that
breezy babe find an All-
American, long-blond-
haired, hippie stud named—
Atticus Rasper?

That was three-quarters
of a lifetime ago.
Since then,

I've survived:
A bat attack,
"Hey Jude," and
Thorazine.

Have screwed
seven beauties,
read the Bible,
kicked Big Brother
in the balls, and
learned to love.

But if that unfinished
Regina business
haunts me still—

I need to get cancer.

what goes down must come up

buried by the buried boy,
beneath the mudslide of miles
of noise,

climbs a punctured heart that will
not die, and when it does reach
the top,

before it topples back,
blood leaks warmly out my eyes—

never am I more alive—

Third Floor

Our next door neighbor was a tall young lady. Denberg was the name on her door. She was raising a little girl and boy alone. Don't know how I knew her first name was Judy. Her boy was nine. Two years younger than me. His name was Jody. An older man moved in with them. The name on the door then read Colello/Denberg. He was a cheap-looking cocka-doodle-doo in a three-quarter black leather coat. Like my father. Across from us lived a well-groomed kid in his late teens with good posture who wore burgundy penny loafers. I thought he might have a classy accent, but he never said boo. I don't recall ever seeing his parents, but was sure the neatly twined stack of books which would sometimes appear by the incinerator chute had belonged to them. Four more doors. In the far corner was a red-headed divorcee and her two kids. Her loner son Steven Stoltz was my age. He was good with dogs and roamed the streets and alleys surrounded by mangy strays. One night his shapely older sister Carol was sitting on our front stoop, her transistor radio blasting something new, "All Day and All of the Night," by The Kinks. The song was exciting. And so was she. Three apartments housed lone old ladies. Two of whom were no longer capable of carrying their chairs downstairs to sit in front of the building. One could, but never did. Her name was Ceil. She knew how to talk to people. And liked my mother. More than once, she would knock on our door and ask, *What's wrong in there?*

A Better Man

She fought them off. Starch-collared, anything-for-
another-lousy-buck jackals, who hungered to disfigure
majestic Grand Central Station. So I'm glad they
renamed The Central Park Reservoir for Jackie O.

On a bench, by that hundred-plus acre body of water,
I soak up some early spring sun. Daydream revelation
and baseball. A merry-go-round of joggers in all shapes
and sizes doggedly run the track which surrounds
the water. A gangly, shaggy-haired kid seats himself
on the track, leisurely leaning against the ornamental
cast-iron fence which separates it from the water.
Hooked up to his iPod, he rolls a smoke. Paperback
in lap. Girlfriend to his left. She's a dark-eyed beauty.
A ballerina. Or a dream. Maybe he's listening to alter-
native rock, maybe Anarchy R Us, while catching up
on some required reading. Maybe he needs all that
simultaneous stimulation because he's a genius. More
likely, he's Holden Caulfield lolling in the luxury of
teenage angst. He absently blows gray bursts of smoke
toward the passing joggers. Maybe the joggers deserve
to be smoked. But why, I wonder, doesn't one kick
the smoke from the self-absorbed twit's hand? And
wonder on...when I hear, "I'm Dan Ingram and I'm
a *better* man than you." Turn to face a crusty old
stranger sitting on the other end of the bench, sporting
a "Korean War Veteran" cap and a happy-drunk grin.
Again he says, "I'm Dan Ingram and I'm a *better* man
than you." "Yeah," I say. "You are a *better* man than me."
Nod toward the kid and add, "But I'm a *better* man than
him." Dan Ingram points at the kid and says, "Him?"
"Yeah," I say. "*Him*. How come it doesn't occur to
him that blowing smoke into gasping joggers' faces
is wrong?" "Simple," says Dan Ingram. "He never got
his ass kicked. Never." And I know he's right. And know
I'm right when I say, "And you know, the amazing thing
is he may never. Ever."

CHINATOWN

Snapping pictures of adulterers in the act is an honest living.
A fine living for fast on his feet, tailored, tough guy,
P.I. Jake Gittes. Smoke. Drink. Joke. And smile, smile, smile
your I'm-in-love-with-myself-so-you-should-be-too smile.
Forget about the girl you couldn't save in Chinatown.

High-class alabaster blonde mindfucker Mrs. Mulwray,
Ida whatever, Walt Disney's mouse...Does it really matter
who hired you to snap shots of Mr. Mulwray with his mistress?
You got paid. It's 30s boomtown L.A.
Forget about the girl you couldn't save in Chinatown.

Why take on venerated old tycoon Noah Cross?
A whale of a man. Creator of his own cash ocean.
That a man is old and made of money does not mean
he no longer needs more—
What are you, Jake, some kind of Red?

Why take on the L. A. Dept. of Water and Power?
The puny big-nosed refugee who blithely switchblade-sliced
your trespassing nose into bloody pulp with a single stroke,
he knows how life plays out in this world of ours.
Forget about the girl you couldn't save in Chinatown.

What's it to you if Noah Cross owns the water supply?

What's it to you if Noah Cross rapes the ghostly 13-year-old
girl he sired raping his daughter, the recently widowed
Mrs. Mulwray?

Mrs. Mulwray is dead. Finely-chiseled face lawfully blown off.

Old Noah Cross. Gnarly and huge. A leafless tree.
Stiff boughs hang tangled over ghostly girl-child shoulders,
clutching her mute open mouth and a teensy naked knee.
Bone-girl. From behind. Reared into his rude trunk.

Cops saw. But only you could taste her sour yellow terror.

Haircut

The traditional peppermint twist pole,
and—$10.00 a cut, plus tip—price,
sold me on Isaac's Best Haircuts Barbershop.

Bolodenka, a gentleman from Uzbekistan,
who spoke little English, did an OK job for me.

Before every haircut I'd say, "Not too short."

After every haircut he'd say, "See you next month."

And so it was, with each month torn from my
2003 Fleet Bank Desk Calendar,
for over a year.

One afternoon—
Comb and scissors clipping my hair in tandem,
he paused *twice* to gaze across the room—
TV game show action.

Bolo, baby,
Zen Buddhists say:
When I eat, I eat.
When I sleep, I sleep.

I say:
When you cut my hair, you cut my hair—
No American-style multi-tasking bullshit.

But, instead, I remained silent.
No need to waste energy.
Fuck Bolodenka!

=

The traditional peppermint twist pole,
and—$12.00 a cut, plus tip—price,
sold me on Executive Barbershop.

Yakov, a gentleman from Russia,
who spoke little English, did an OK job for me.

Before every haircut I'd say, "Not too short."

After every haircut he'd try to sell me conditioner.

And so it was, with each month torn from my
2004 Fleet Bank Desk Calendar,
for over a year.

One afternoon—
Comb and scissors clipping my hair in tandem,
Three muffled musical notes buzzed into our air—
He paused, reached for the cell phone,
and tucked it between his left shoulder and ear.
Yammering Russian and clipping my hair.

Yakov, baby,
Zen Buddhists say:
When I eat, I eat.
When I sleep, I sleep.

I say:
When you cut my hair, you cut my hair—
No American-style multi-tasking bullshit.

But, instead, I remained silent.
No need to waste energy.
Fuck Yakov!

            =

Up in the Bronx,
there was Foo's Gift Shop, on Belmont.
Mr. Foo sold bags and backpacks,
porcelain elephant plant stands,
and replaced watch batteries.

In back, was a metal folding chair.
On which, I sat. Relaxed—

As a dark-eyed,
orange butterfly, fluttered above me.
Snipping a song—for $8.00 flat.

GRACE

I liked you and your
unsmiling, ghetto bred,
Hungarian father
a lot.

His huge head of black curls,
leaden handshake, retiring dark
eyes, and Popeye forearms.

That he seemed partial to
short sleeves, unashamed
of his numerical, blurry, blue
Auschwitz tattoo.

And you, Grace,
a studious cherry rice pudding,
behind Coke bottle granny glasses,
hopeful, oceanic gray eyes—

Told me your father firmly replied
no thanks, he'd rather stay home and
rest than accept your offer to treat
him to *Fiddler on the Roof* for his
birthday.

You suspected he really
did not know
the true date of his birth.

He told you his full-bearded, orthodox
father had toiled as a chairmender,
and he himself pressed garments at the
dry cleaning plant.
But you...

The way he watched out for you
was right.

Silently,
sizing me up as I played it cool
on Kuklemonga Street.

Staring back, I noticed that his tattoo
started with a triangle.

I hope
he survived to see his baby Grace
become a scholar and a mother,
moving from the Bronx to Wisconsin
and on to Haifa.

And know you burn too,
knowing there's a viral-eyed,
squeaky Ahmadinejad who
says your father never existed.

19 Actions More Practical than Writing this Poem

Assaulting the wall with my head. Switching to a raw food diet.
Curing cat co-dependency. Channeling Elvis. Blaming the messenger.
Playing computer solitaire. Playing lotto. Playing the kazoo.
Petitioning the lord with prayer. Massaging my prostate.
Assaulting the wall with *your* head. Reading Thackeray's Vanity Fair.
Taking up golf. Dancing the Funky Chicken. Shaving my chest.
Casting a vote for American Idol. Collecting Nazi war memorabilia.
Shouting Bama Lama, Bama Loo. Netting butterflies. Collecting dust.

TOMMY BOLAN

The raggy, rage-filled voice of my father spasmed noise
to match the noise made, as he harshly shoved kitchen
furniture on the linoleum floor—

    to get to mom?

I—was a little kid, in the darkness of my bed—her cries
were muffled—the door stayed closed, I couldn't sleep—

    was he hitting her?

My little sister slept in the other bed. It was the only
bedroom of the 3 room apartment. On the other side of the
shut door was a small foyer. To the left was the bathroom.
On the right was the doorless arched entrance to the living
room—where our parents would sleep on the sofa bed. You
had to pass through the living room to get to the kitchen.
If I dared go out—it might stop. Sometimes my mother
would come into my room sweaty and scared and sleep with me.
And we slept. Months might have passed between beatings,
but the threat was—always—there.

So, I'd get up to piss a lot and stay up and go out and
come back and do what my mother told me to do and years
passed and I kept an eye out and I went out to look at the
girls who loved me but I had no good clue about and while
I was out—he stabbed her dead—and she was gone, and he
was gone straight to jail—and my sister and I now had to
go live with our maternal grandparents and they were old
and infirm and I kept an eye out for them and—it started—
the most ordinary thing—a short passage from a book—
over and over in my head increasingly and replaced by another
series of numbers increasingly I was crazy—of course—
look who my father was. And liquor made me feel better and
liquor and pills made it better to feel nothing and I felt
nothing when I OD'ed at 16, and it *was* better. I should know.

THE VOLUNTEER

Steaming in the August stench of Times Square,
my co-worker and I scooted and sidled through
the stylish rush hour roil of office workers,
when she turned to me and, through whiter than
white teeth, said:

"I believe in giving something back, so I'm on
my way to St. Ignatius's Church. Tonight is my
night to serve supper to the homeless."

"That's kind of you," I said.

"What about you?" she asked.
"What do you do?"

"I never got anything,
so I've got nothing to give back."

Unfazed, she turned away.
We walked on, side by side.

Amid the swarming sidewalk stood a copper-
colored, short and sturdy, gray-braided woman
wearing a sandwich board sign: *Men's Suits—
Blowout Sale!*

She held out flyers for passersby. As though
she were a fire hydrant, all passed her by.
I stepped over to her. Face glistened metallic
sweat. Took a flyer and said, "Thank you."

For This, You Motherfuckers Will Not Be Getting 70 Virgins

There, on the wailing wall at Grand Central:

MISSING
since 9-11

Smile of a birthday boy—

A brown Buddha this young man Clyde Bevins Junior,

The kind of guy who would never abandon his old mama
to a nursing home,

A messenger planning to study architecture—

"Not a bad bone in his body," said a Stork Messenger
Service co-worker, of his fellow Mets fan.

A man born to be the good father!

"EVERY MORNING I SEE YOU SMILING, I MISS YOU,
WE NEVER MET."

On a card taped next to his picture,
anonymously—

DAMON'S WAY

1 operable
pay phone in this
uptown burned
down 'hood and
this large shoul-
dered crack dealer is
dominating it.
his hooded lookout
hangs loose and their un-
leashed pit bull stays:
ugly. waiting for
the phone,

damon, is as sig-
nificant to the
ambitious dealer
—as say—that
passing stray, white,
black-pawed cat.

damon
takes a quick
last glance at the
grinning dealer and
starts turning, to split
—NOW—

that cat—is
—CRUNCHED—instantly:
broken, muted, and
limp—in the indust-
rial locked jaws
of the bucket head-
ed 50 lb. pit,
the pit, collared
has—now—been
suspended

in air "the cat
started it!" blurts
the dealer, phone-
less, as he and his
lookout incred-
ulously witness

damon dangling their
gurgling cat crunching
pit in mid-air,
twisting

its collar
violently
to cut the pit's
air. looking, arms
length from his
taut bruce lee bo-
dy damon wonders—
when did I grab this
killer pit?
60

seconds later the
choked pit un-
locks and drops the
broken backed collapsed
but not very
bloody barely breath-
ing cat, to the

pavement, and
damon tosses the
whimpering
pit to the pave-
ment, and man

nor dog did
shit, as damon laid
the small mass of cat
into the flat back
of his double-parked
2-door rusting
gray toyota hatch-
back starlet, and

ran many lights
on the way to the
24 hours a
day emergency
drop-off at the

ASPCA
on 1st avenue
by 89th street,
and in his
heart he
knew

the cat had not
many breaths left,
and when they got there—
he saw, that the bro-
ken backed collapsed cat
had belly

crawled up, and was
curled beside
him, and damon was
moved to let the cat
die right there,
with dignity—
by his side, but
instead,

opted to do
his "duty,"
to take the cat
inside, where,
maybe—they could op-
erate, and the cat—
survive. the dying
cat

strengthless struggled
against damon's
arms, struggled
to stay, in—
the car. in the A
SPCA

a volun-
teer took the broken
backed collapsed cat from
damon's arms and
laid it into a
too small cage,
even if the cat

—could've—stood
it wouldn't have been
able to in that
too small cage,
and as the volun-

teer whisked the
cat to the back
room damon wit-
nessed the cat quake,
and as damon left,
he crumblestuffed the
receipt he'd gotten
for the cat into
the left pocket of
his jeans, where he kept
—only—his keys, on
a ring, and half

an hour
later he called
and was told the
cat quaked
20 minutes
straight and
died, and damon
got

down, on himself—
for not letting
the cat die, with
dignity—
by his side, and
as damon wiped vo-
mitbloodshit from the
black vinyl flat back
of his hatchback

thunder-
ous self-hatred wreaked
merciless havoc.

this last fact is
one key in un-
derstanding damon's
impulsive act, of

homeric courage—
bare handedly
rescuing the cat
—out—the deathlock
jaws of the infer-
nal bucket-headed
beast, something

you, nor anyone
you've ever met—
would, or could—
do.

HURLY-BURLY BUROO

—A concoction created to ward off a five-time draft
deferred, shotgun toting, septuagenarian reptile clad
in an orange vest.

asshole of a tarantula
low john root
10 yenta tongues
wattle of a rooster
essence of a rose
clit ring of a whore
wahoo root bark
sumac berries
Ed Bradley's earring
underbelly of a wild boar
ingrown toenail of a centenarian
90 milligrams methadone
eyeball of a Cyclops
Mr. Potato Head
tonsils of Deep Throat
a partridge and a pear tree
foreskin of an elephant
heart of a flea
wallet of a schnorr
broom straws
1 Big Mac
2 hunchbacks
hot licks and deer ticks
whiskers of a hipster
left testicle of a sex addict
entrails of a sewer rat
violet leaf
liver of a sot
a purring furry cat

12 pints blood /
from any billionaire real estate developer
sprinkle MSG
and

boil it all in a pot.

Boychick Exquisite

Looking up from my crib,
I saw a small stuffed tiger
being handed down to me.
Somehow—
I knew it belonged to me.

Maybe,
I had played with it before.
I don't remember.

Firstborn,
and,
a boy child:
I struck grandma's hand with
my toy guitar,
my dark hair turned blond,
the blow broke her finger,
my mother let my loose curls
grow long I
looked like a girl—
I don't remember.

Grandma would show-off her
crooked finger to me.

I remember—
calling for my mother,
while running to the toilet—
and waiting for her—
jumping around,
and waiting.
A boychick exquisite—
I had blessed her.

HEARTS TO CLUBS

"I'm out,"

says Milt, the father of our host, as he folds his cards. Bloated and wasted, in his fifties, he's about thirty years older than me and the three other players seated around the table. He turns to his son who's still in. He tells him:

"Ya dunno watda fuck ya doin' an' it's fuckin' ME up."

His son doesn't even look at him. He's locked in on the pot. Milt splashes some cologne on his scalp and combs his three hairs straight back. Broke. He rises. And heads to the toilet.

Seven card poker. In the single-room Bronx basement apartment. On the bicentennial.

Campbell deals the final round—down. Clockwise, to those players still in the pot: our host, Philip, me, and himself. Our host pulls his cards slow and opens with a buck bet. Looks left at who's next—and says to him:

"It's to you Philip FuckinRetard."

Philip laughs nervously. He babbles. Campbell yells at him:

"Shutdafuckup!"

He does—but not before he ups the bet another buck. It's to me—there's about forty bucks in the pot. I need to squeeze a heart for a flush—any heart—I need to squeeze a heart—a heart to the hearts—a heart to the hearts— a heart—

"Ya inna out?"
—Clubs—

TARANTULA DANCE

He walks on water,
has 8 eyes,
8 relentless long legs,
1" fangs,

and forges over
miles of jungle land,

following her wind-
blown mating scent
to its source—

the silk of her burrow.

There,
his hairy black ball
body vibrates
a trilling invitation
while front legs stamp
a rhythmic shiver
of need...

She emerges—
a brown mirror image
of him.

Not immune
to his own poison,
he approaches hot
with cold caution.

She has been known
 to change her mind—

might kill and eat him.

He holds her.
She holds him.

Gently, he taps her—
ta-ta-ta-ta-taps...

Sixteen intertwined
spindly legs sway this
way and that—
ta-ta-ta-ta-taps...

Sixty plus minutes,
till she's slack in a trance.

Seed planted...
he flees for his life.

Myles Spenser

Passed out. Died. Dope OD. Twenty-three. My powerful, round body was carried out of the shooting gallery into the South Bronx sunlight, laid out by the front stoop and abandoned. One block from where I grew up.

The old man loved dope. After decades of dope, he settled for methadone, a part-time gig driving a limo, and J&B Whisky. The old lady yelled at the walls. She was heavy into bingo. I got a younger brother, Jay. A nickel-and-dime methadone addict. I tried to throw him out a window for…I forget what. Don't remember ever caring about any of them.

The year I turned 23, moved to a better neighborhood. There, I met Baker. Dug him. Handed him a bag of pot and told him to take as much as he wanted. Told him how the hit-and-run left me with a steel-pin in my hip and glass eye. And if anyone ever bothered him, to let me know—because I don't expect to make 25.

I fucked-up a huge Fordham U. football player outside a nightclub. I fucked-up a pimp, poolside, in Miami. I let Eddie Thomas get the better of me, because I liked him—and he was right.

I ate it up when Baker and the boys would go on about great I was, and loved to hear my deep, sweet voice talk them up.

The boys shot dope. I dove in. I ripped-off a dealer. Pulled him right out from behind the wheel of his van. We all got-off on the roof. I mugged an old man, bloodied his fine blue pinstriped Sunday suit.

I shot big hits. The day my dead body was found, I shot a lot of good-shit.

Jay Spenser

I needed that token clerk job. So, I stepped up to the urinal next to where some chump was pissin'—and took it. Stuck my plastic cup under his piss—and took it. He ran out, the faggot. HA-HA! Washed my hands. My own urine was dirty, and I wouldn't have got the job. Piss I hijacked got me that job.

A piss I took a couple years before that almost got me killed. A bunch of us were up at Baker's. I was feelin' real nice on extra meth and sprayed weed. So I follow my girl, Bernice, into the bathroom where she sits on the pot to piss—and does. Stand over her, so I can piss between her legs—and do. All the time we're laughin', and a couple guys come in and watch and laugh and watch—

This flips my crazy ass-kickin' brother Myles out. He comes blowin' in from the livin' room and grabs me by my hair and throat. My dick still out—drippin'—he drags me into the livin' room. Tries to throw me out the sixth floor window. Didn't like what I was doin' with Bernice. If it was Slow Boat or Baker doin' it—guys he liked—he wouldn't have cared. Might've laughed. But it was me. It took 3 guys and a screamin' Bernice to save my life.

All that goes back…gotta be 5-6 years. Myles died—OD. Then ma dropped dead at the bingo hall—heart attack. And last year, the old man's liver finally gave. I didn't go claim his body at the city morgue. Fuck it. He was dead, and I needed cash. Cash—gonna get kicked out this rathole if I don't kick in to that junkie bitch Connie. Shit—I used to get foxy chicks. Twenty-eight come May—look like shit. A bony goat's ghost. Feel like shit. Bad as when I was flat on my back at Bronx Lebanon—starin' crazy pain at ceilin', nose broke, kickin' smack—alone. Wished I was dead. Well, I'm alone. But now I ain't on my back. I'm goin'—out her window. The sixth floor—the same floor Myles tried to throw me from. HA-HA! Only this time it's on my own. And piss—got nothin' to do with it.

The President's Daughter Caught a Big Fish in Kennebunkport

Third straight Thursday 3:00 p.m. lunch break,
at the counter of Primo's Diner, down on Broadway—

Same brunette waitress, with the odd eyes
(one fierce and blue, the other lazy, filmy-gray),
Betty Boop boobs,
and Eastern European accent.

"Hi!" I say.

"Hello," she replies.

"I'll have a tuna salad platter, coffee, and water."

Flip through the first few pages of the Daily News—
She returns with the coffee and water.

"I'm Ted."

"I am Petra."

"Is that Russian?"

"Polish."

"Oh, my mother was from Poland. Polish Jew.
Called me Tadeusz."

"Tadeusz, Petra...These are good names, yes?"

"Yes."

Cecil Beaton beckons for a coffee refill—
She scurries off.
Flip through the rest of the paper, sip coffee...

Petra returns with the ample tuna salad platter.
Which includes: potato salad, cucumber, tomato,
2 packets of Melba toast, coleslaw, and a hard-boiled egg,
 spread on a bed of lettuce. Sets it gently down before me.

Casting her blue eye at my Daily News, she asks—
"What is news?"

"The president's daughter caught a big fish in Kennebunkport."

She laughs, throatily.

Silently, picks up a packet of my Melba toast.
Long nurturing fingers flawlessly tear open the cellophane.
She consecrates the second packet similarly. All—

For me.

And I want to say something warm—
Something wonderful—

But I've got a mouthful of potato salad—

Then she was gone.

A Lion is a Cow

Meat I ate was once a lion.
Had to be. My mother told me
it would make me strong.
Like a lion.

She'd cut it up for me, into
little pieces. I'd leave the last
piece. She'd say: the last
piece was the key.

Years later: I learned,
meat I ate was not a lion.
I was: hurtshocked.
A cow?

the sweetest dream

climaxed in
iris—
we slept,
I dreamt:

            candy colored
          baby birds—

               afloat

         in flight—

                snowflakes
              of song—

          like

             notes of
                lovelight—

        like—

looking up,
from my crib—
at a mobile—

           wide-eyed

Dealing in Prayer
(at 26)

Lift—*1—18—2—9—?? 1—18—*
this—*1—18—2—9—20—18—1—18—25*
curse—*1—18—2—??*—from me.
God—this
1—18—2—9—20—18—1—18—25
CLATTEREXACT
jack—*1—18—??*—hammer
1—18—2—9—20—18—1—18—25
Mind demolisher
And—*1—18—2—9—?? 1—18—2—9—20?*
I will never beg another favor.
1—18—2—9—20—18—1—18—25
1—18—2—9—20—18—1—18—25
1—18—2—9—20—??

Having no faith to pray:

PLEASE HEAR MY PLEAS TO DEAL!
*1—18—2—9—*And I will—*1—18—*
never beg—*2—9—20—18—1—18—25*
—another favor. *1—18—2—9—??*

And my upper lip swelled,

1—18—2—9—20—18—1—18—25
1—18—?? 1—18—2—9?
1—18—2—9—20—18—1—18—25

And my body stiffened,

1—18—2—9—??
1—18—2—9—20—18?

I lay listless nine days.

On the tenth day I arose
And realized, that
As I lay stricken, the curse had been
Lifted.

And I said to Him:

> I have known the curse that has been
> Lifted.
>
> And I will never beg another favor.
> And I will hide and not be cursed
> Again.

WHITE MEN IN SANDALS

On the Fahrenheit scale the boiling point of water is 212.
On the Fahrenheit scale the all-white-men-in-Manhattan-slip-into-sandals point is 55.

In low white Cons I ran for my life real fast across Bronx concrete.
In steel-tipped black boots I stood fast and kicked shin-cracking low.
In high-gloss black police oxfords I passed as an off-duty cop.
Today, in black New Balance walking shoes, I walk Manhattan.
They have taken over.

Foul-footed exhibitionists,
unprepared for fight or flight.

Men from Idaho with enormous feet.
Men from France with itsy-bitsy feet.
Men from Long Island with filthy feet.
A John Ashbery acolyte with cloven feet.

As though there were a date with Miss Japan at stake, they patiently wait in long lines at trendy City Bakery, breaking out the plastic to pay $12.50 per pound to lunch on slightly above average salad bar crap from a paper plate.

Sans the support of innersoles they subway to Yankee Stadium. Taking in the art deco Grand Concourse, which they will invade. Turning live poultry markets into vintage clothes shops and the saint-haven botanicas into pet spas.

Deep auto exhaust inhalers, they dine at upscale sidewalk cafes, viewing scenic black mountain ranges of rancid garbage packed 58-gallon plastic trash bags, and a parade of shitting dogs. Why not just toss a tablecloth over the hood of a parked Buick?

Always ready to hop the jitney to Southampton.

Maybe someday, I too, will let my doggies breathe.

REDEMPTION

Don't remember any Little League team names,
not even the one I was on. Nor do I remember
the coach or manager or whatever he was called,
except that there *was* one, and his doofus son
played first base. We played at Grenadier Field.
That I'm sure of. Because I remember warming
the bench and wondering who was this Grenadier
guy? I quickly concluded he was a dead man
who had always worn a suit and tie to work.
Except for Beaver's father, Mr. Cleaver, on TV,
I had never seen such a man. It seemed unnatural,
punishing even. Like going to a funeral every day...
although, I was certain these were the men who
made sure all was right in the world and dictated
important letters to pretty secretaries.

Anyway, I showed up for a game or two, was
a late-inning replacement in right field, made an
error, and struck out in my sole turn at bat. Some
boys already knew how to hit and field more than
a little. Figured they were born knowing, which
made me a retard, so I never went back. And that
was that. Then I started watching the Mets like
Cleon Jones and Tommie Agee, and after a while
I picked up on their technique—how they'd watch
the ball all the way to the bat and generate power
and bat speed throughout the hips.

Five thousand plus Major League Baseball games
later, I'd often watch the Yankees with my 11-year-
old niece, Amanda, who proudly wore their team
cap. I'd point stuff out. Other times we'd practice
some. Play catch. Then I'd pitch, she'd hit, and I'd
fetch. So when her softball Raptors were up one and
the dreaded Sea Horses had the tying and winning
runs at the corners with two out in the bottom of the
ninth and a hard grounder was hit to her at third base,
she began the catching-moving-throwing movement
as it approached, moving her feet to get to it and icily
arced a long sidearm throw across the diamond to
first--to beat the runner by a full stride! Coach and
teammates all whooped it up while just outside the
third base line I stomped and waved a fist shouting,
"Yeah, Amanda! Yeah, yeah, yeah! Way to go!"

SALAMANDERS

How he got pinned Woim or why, none of us
knew. He looked regular enough. Like any one
of us slightly older teenaged boys who also lived
in the projects. Fact is, we didn't know or care
what his real name was, or if he even had one.

One day, out of the blue, he approaches us and
boldly says, "I don't go by *that name* anymore."
As if he ever had a choice in the matter. "Okay...
Woim." He must've been about 17 when I heard
that he got drunk and drowned at Orchard Beach.

Following every summer rain thereafter, a putrid
odor of unknown origin would rise and linger in
the projects and the grounds would be littered with
wriggling worms. Figured it somehow had to do
with the death of Woim, but kept that to myself.

Decades later, the cool air soothed as I walked
through a lush park following a summer rain. Trees
and flowers...but most pleasing was that there was
no else around. I felt a sense of wonder. Like when
I was a little boy in the Catskills after a summer rain...

The cool air smelled green. Tingling mist tickled.
On the dirt road by the woods tiny orange dragons
appeared. Soft yellow-underbellies. But when I
stepped out of the park onto the busy city street,
for no apparent reason Woim popped into my head.

He'd been dead a year or so, when I learned the girl
I was out on a date with was his sister. Pretty, with
waist-length black hair, Joanna wore a white sundress.
She seemed obsessed with St. Francis of Assisi. As
far as obsessions went, I figured, a damn good one.

At the movies we saw actors dot vast wheat fields in
Days of Heaven. She smelled of garlic, but I didn't care.
Said she was devoutly Catholic like her Puerto Rican
mom. Her father, a Czech gypsy, had long since aban-
doned them. Joanna Redzosko...Woim...Redzosko.

Simeon

Joseph was our old father's favorite,
whom all ten of his brothers hated.

A too-precious-to-shepherd-with-us
seventeen-year-old dreamer,
who'd stroll about in his multicolored coat
that the great old man had bestowed upon him.

Hubris-filled and foolish, he
boldly announced his dreams—
of our obeisance to him...!

Camped far from our land of Hebron,
we ten fed father's abundant flock of sheep—
when the dreamer appeared.

As natural as the river runs—
we would slaughter the favored son.

Tip his carcass into a deep dark pit.

"No bloodstains!" Reuben exclaimed.

From Joseph's unblemished back—
we tore the multicolored coat.
Screaming murderously, he kicked up a storm.
But as though he were a dung-packed sack—
we slung him—and he plummeted down—

Let him *dream* his death!

A Jewish Giant at Home with his Parents in the Bronx, N.Y. 1970

On the photograph by Diane Arbus

bare bulb in a wall lamp
tall vertical rectangular wall moldings
plaster streaked ceiling cracks
slip-covered club chairs and couch
plastic covered lampshades
freshly vacuumed old carpet
lackluster curtains (closed)
2 generic paintings and
a console TV

But foremost—upright! An untapped continent. An oxygen-inhaling colossus.
Perfectly proportioned. Complete with horse's neck and tree trunk wrists.

But why brother, why?

Sorely stooped and donning the mocking mask of the eternally defeated?

Of me? You?! Asks the electrified face of the frumpy little yenta, glare fixed
high—on her son.

At her shoulder, the small and formal father spaces: *Pinochle by Hy's at seven
o'clock.* Hands in pockets, he absently faces his son's abdomen. Resigned to this
picture-taking monkey business.

My dear giant:
I'd lay 2 to 1 you don't need that cane and orthopedic shoe,
nor slingstone and faith in Yahweh to have slain Goliath.
Shake the dead weight of days from your nuclear shoulders.
Tell *them* you're going out job-hunting.
Fuck one hundred hardcore hookers.
Bust some heads that need busting—

> unleash the fury
> unleash the fury
> unleash the fury,
>
> unleash the love

GOD'S HONEY

Bred to shop, she bled on God.
And was guided by His signs to her.

exquisite
gold blizzard
woolen curls
liquid sky
blue eyes she
stood long arms
sides holy
bible tight
in right hand
pearl white silk
button-down
blouse unbut-
toned shawl-like
over nar-
row shoulders
draped upper
back slack sleeves
fell past slight
breasts slender
presence weight-
less angel
sequined cream
body shirt—
black velvet
hip huggers—
naked neck
natural
scented swan—

Could tell, by talk she'd talk,
daddy was a millionaire—
Could tell, by her walk in my heart,
she should have been around
when Jesus walked—following him—

A sparrow on each of her bony shoulders—

The Essential Dentistry of Dr. Jack Kreeger

Former Bronx Golden Gloves
bantamweight contender,
toothless and fit, old Dr. Jack Kreeger
is the last affordable dentist.

Mirthful, manic-laugh-loud,
he floats around his spacious office
calling all men "my brother" and all
women "my sister" or "princess."

Refuses to wear a mask, refers all
root canals out, and has the genius to
surround himself with beauty—
an all-peachy Puerto Rican girl
intern and office staff.

Ambitious dental-hygienist,
silky, sing-song-speaking Gloria
drills my upper right bicuspid.

Next week, Dr. Kreeger will extract
my throbbing lower left molar,
without the standard, self-serving
teeth will shift dental bullshit.

"Beautiful! Beautiful!" shouts Dr. Kreeger,
exhaling Beef Lo Mein breath
directly into my wide open mouth
as he reviews Gloria's work up close.

I agree.

Eyeballing the rope-like scar across
my neck and having heard my breathy
rasp, he earnestly asks,
"Teddy, my brother, what happened?"

So I tell him.

He replies, "That they got everything,
is all that matters."

Seizing the pity price moment I pounce,
"Yeah, but I have exorbitant medical bills."

"Listen motherfucker," he chortles,
"you're lucky to be alive!"

The Day Before Christmas

Dumped horizontal, curbside,
between the high-rent high-rise
and my orphan heart,
a long, conical, dark-green-needled pine,
on a frozen bank of auto-exhaust-frosted black snow.

Did they get their dates mixed up?
Upgrade to a bigger one?
Want you to think you've got your dates mixed up?

Or what?

Professor Stephen Niemeyer

This morning they came for the books. Two bearded young men, their hands filled with shopping bags. Five large mahogany bookcases full. Mathematics. And the treasures of my late beloved wife, Maria. Music and literature. Eighty with arthritic hips, I am resigned to be moving to a first-rate assisted-living facility. Except for some seminal volumes I removed and stacked to the side, I told them all books go. Over and done with. Payment received. Not that I *need* the money. Nor am I pressed to vacate. But scheduling weeks in advance in order for the university or a charity to pick up tripped my screw-up detector. No space for a library and of course less privacy. Sentimentality does not serve me. Maria gone and our son and his growing family thriving in Iowa. What an old fool I am keeping our family tradition of a Christmas tree. On this day before Christmas I insisted that the young beards dispose of the tree. They also took the book stack I had placed to the side. Probably felt entitled since I made them take the tree.

ONE DAY IN NOVEMBER

Carafe of black coffee.

Tweak a villanelle. Read *The Complete Idiot's Guide to Reinventing Yourself.*

Turn on clock radio. A possessed man shouts his truth: "ALTHOUGH RESULTS MAY
VARY YOU HAVE NO CHOICE BUT TO LOSE WEIGHT WHEN TAKING FAT
ABSORB NO CHOICE!"—

Take half a nap. Take a piss. Complete the nap.

Gulping OJ, plan my day—a leisurely walk through Central Park to the P.O.

On the street engage—posted atop her stoop—old wheelchair-bound widow Julia about
how she fared playing the slots in AC.

At the park's archway entrance, a rakish dachshund and a yawping cross between a
Pekinese and a fly wrestle each other into an ass-sniffing knot.

Walk in. Walk on…kick back on a bench. Flawlessly clashing Fall colors. Dread black
at five. The brown 9x12 envelope resting on my lap contains my screenplay contest entry
and sacrificial $15.00 reading fee. Oh well…

owe it to myself. Still,

should have sprinkled anthrax on the manuscript. And what's this puny plaque affixed to
backrest of bench? Bestowed by Mr. and Mrs. Leo Bagatelle? What?! The city can't
afford to pay for its own benches? Why couldn't the Bagatelles spray-paint their tag onto
a subway car? And why should I need to see my name crawl across some yummy
starlet's nakedness?

Why not?

Relax shoulders. God's cool air caresses nostrils. Flows in and out and in and out and in
and out…flushing head. Like a shadow, slip out of myself. And watch…

Letter to Lori Waterhouse
for Amy Foster

The tip off: When, outside your ventilator- and sole daughter-dependent, old mother's hospital room, you cast unblinking, glazed, rainbow-green eyes on yours truly and your longtime friend Judith (don't call me Judy) Pizzutti, and said, "I probably shouldn't say this, but you two look good together." And so, I became a burnt offering. But really, Judith Pizzutti?! Joyce Starr…maybe. Yeah, Miss Starr. Star…like the star-saturated, boundless, black sky we marveled at that late August night in Ogunquit as we lay supine in chaise lounges on the back lawn side by side. Falling meteoroids turned into trails of blazing light in our atmosphere. Thirty-three murky years since I had last seen even a single star, until that night we shared. Rebirthed, beneath the four-and-a-half-billion-year-old night light of Cassiopeia, Hank Williams, and you—my aurora Lori. Last night I dreamt I awoke and saw your doll face with my one open (left) eye—and felt warm inside, knowing you were replenishing yourself sleeping safely by my side. But I must confess, I long ago discarded my fleece-lined, ear-flapped, green camouflage L.L. Bean hunting cap we got to match. But hope I've held on to a few of the IQ points I gained from the forehead-to-forehead osmosis. And still have your (no longer state of the art) video camera that you never asked me to return. And the *whys* of my immortal love could roll easily on off my fat tongue, but the prevalent reason for this epistle is to *tell you* something I may otherwise *never* get the chance to. That is, in retrospect, how quietly clear it is that I was the compact and rather suave Gomez to your wonderfully aloof and statuesque Morticia. John Astin and Carolyn Jones, the original TV version of course. And like Gomez, I would have planted kisses from your fingertips to your shoulder on your most accessible arm several times each and every day. So I'm telling you *now*.

The Healing

Last night I killed my father. A garrote. Pulled his neck back with the force of a TV set falling from a 6-story rooftop and his legs flew up and he landed flat on his back. Dead before he hit the floor, he never saw it coming. Did him in the very bedroom of my conception. I don't recall a thud.

TO THE LIGHT, DARKLY

News that Bill Gates is no
longer the world's richest man
shook me.

I was moved to contemplate
man's place in the universe.
God's accordion.

Our tiny mortal minds are
hard-wired for linear time.

Time exists only relative
to constant speed of light.
Einstein's violin.

Mind is a sense.
Like sight, taste, hearing,
smell, and touch.
No more, no less.

Because I think I am?
Am what?

Parting the flooded Jordan River
was God's final meddle into
men's affairs.

Minor personal miracles occur:
Deeds of dangling spirits of dead.

In time we die.

Like my neighbor down the hall,
Mrs. Scirghio, said after her husband
died choking on a chicken bone:

"When ya numbuz up, ya numbuz up."

Eternity is a conceit.

Absence of time
is not eternity.

Every breath is.

Straight Lines

My mother said I should be afraid of my own shadow. My father said I should ram my fist deep down a big wet red dog's throat. A dignified old lady neighbor said I was a nice boy. Go fuck yourself, I replied. Hot shit Petey Cooney said I was real shit because I dropped a pop fly. Miss Pakula said I was smart in school. The palmist took one long look at my palm, said nothing. Stared sadly at me, and split. My grandmother said I was a doppelganger. My grandfather who escaped the Nazis, said I was a Nazi. Mike Gucci at 7 Santini Bros. Moving & Storage Co. said I couldn't do anything right. The white detective with the yellow eyes said the many teeth marks on the dead girl's broken body were mine. My Uncle Saul said I should flee to Israel. My Uncle Jerry said I should go to law school and get married. A state appointed Pakistani psychiatrist said I was a paranoid schizophrenic. Alison Katz said my dick was too small. Alison Katz said my dick was too big. A Korean hooker said I had a nice dick. The most guarded person I've ever met, said I was the most guarded person he's ever met. Lucy Reyes said I was talented, had a full head of hair, and knew how to treat a lady. Helen Bannister said I was the most horrible man she'd ever met. An old friend said I had nothing to die or live for. Said my poetry was old and tired. That I need to bathe regularly and get a girlfriend. *Whatever you say.*

Stories

From the Diary of a Prizefighter

In all twenty-six years of my life the government never did shit for me. And that's OK. But I will not allow them to be business partners of mine. Today, in 1983, I work only for me. Nights, in a four-door 74 Ford Fairmont which I turned into a gypsy cab a few months after coming out of a weeklong coma.

The coma shut-down my promising boxing career. I was an up-and-coming white middleweight with a professional record of 8-0, when less than thirty seconds into my first fight on cable TV, a four-round preliminary match in Vegas, that plodding Panamanian deliberately head-butts me right above my left eye. Blinded bloody instantly, I couldn't see the right-hook into my chin that immediately followed. And the referee sees this head-butt as unintentional.

Anyway, this cab business suits me okay. I'm my own boss. I call no man boss. It's against nature, or my nature. Working nights, less people around. And that's good, because something about most everyone bothers me. Especially, if they bring up that fight. Like the other day, I'm walking on Broadway and a sprightly old-timer approaches me. "Aren't you?" he starts to ask, before I cut him off—

"Look," I say, down into his obviously many times broken old nose, "I don't know you, and you don't know me. Let's keep it that way." The hurt look in his eyes...he probably was an ex-fighter. For the rest of the day, I couldn't shake it.

It's not like I've got anyone else to support—so the money's okay. Six nights, ten till six. I don't knock myself out working long shifts. Knock myself out? HA!

I cruise Upper Manhattan, Harlem, and the South Bronx. This includes Washington Heights, the Dominican neighborhood where I live.

My work starts with a pick up of whores from ghetto rooming-houses and residential hotels on West 145th Street, in Black Harlem. I shuttle them to Hunts Point, an industrial part of the South Bronx just a quick trip across the Harlem River, connected to the south-east Bronx by a short bridge.

Having grown-up down in Manhattan's Meatpacking District, nothing was new to me. So I knew, because of their size and Adam's apples, that many of these full-breasted girls were actually chicks with dicks. Chicks, or chicks with dicks, no matter. No tip. But they are regular business.

Anyhow, as far as the chicks with dicks—considering all the shit they have to go through—I respect their commitment to perversity. Besides—as far as I'm concerned—a blow-job is a blow-job is a blow-job. Anyway you cut it. Cut it?! HA! I'm glad mine wasn't!

During the winter months open bonfires burn in corners of block long vacant lots in the wholesale fruit market that is Hunts Point. Fires surrounded by gatherings of warming whores. The whores wait for cruising johns, who pull up in cars and trucks, to signal them in. How do they fuel their ceaseless all-night bonfires? Coats open to showcase bare hormone tits, they shake their bodies around for more warmth. As though they were possessed by thousands of live tongues of lizards—while their fire burns like bright, flashing, orange razors. Smoke rising into cold gray.

Sometimes, I feel like joining these amazingly tall stiletto-heeled warriors in their supernatural shimmy surrounding their fire. Maybe we could pull one of these doughy faced johns from his car and toss his flabby ass into the fire and dance and scream in exaltation, muffling his cries. And if he survived, he'd have the burn scars for the rest of his fucking life. A constant reminder of how, on a cold winter's night in the South Bronx, a black tribe of chicks with dicks along with a titless white prick fed him to their roaring bonfire. What fucking shame. Like getting knocked into a coma on TV?

A couple nights a week local men gather at Hunts Point job sites, in order to get work unloading crates of fruit from incoming tractor trailers. The pay is five dollars per hour, only about a third of what I net driving, but in order to stay in some kind of shape and share in the camaraderie I often join them. Really, I need to start roadwork again. And then the gym. Or maybe I'll apply to City College and take up writing, journalism maybe. Hell, I bet I've read a lot more than most of these college kids.

After knocking off from an unloading shift at two a.m. one night I noticed a very-slow moving station wagon passing by. On its roof, stacked but not tied down, were wooden pallets. Those used to hold the crates of fruit while in the truck, and then discarded by the truckers after the unloading. From about thirty hazy yards, I now observed the station wagon lazily pulling over at a corner curbside gathering of whores by a dying bonfire. I took two steps closer, and squinting, observed a black man in an ankle-length down coat and a furry ear-flapped hunting cap emerge from the driver's seat into the cold. He shoved the unbound pallets off the roof of his station wagon. Onto the sidewalk, crashed the wooden load. The guy looked to be about the same height as me, five-ten. But even factoring out the bulky coat, I could tell that he was exceptionally broad. In exchange for the pile of pallets he was handed some bills by a towering, open-coated (to showcase big bare tits), dicked chick. As the deliverer of pallets turned to get back into the car the street-light struck his face so that I recognized him as Kent. A hard-bodied wall of a fortyish guy I'd run into at the nearby 24-hour Dominican bodega. He'd often be standing up front, looking out, while killing time sipping from a container of coffee. Now I knew why I'd sometimes see him buy several packs of various brands of cigarettes, assorted junk food, and small bottles of under-the-counter Dominican rum. I don't recall who initiated the salutations originally, but we would exchange "hey mans."

"Hey man," I said while approaching him in the bodega the very next night.

"Hey man," replied Kent. He had one of those naturally gravelly voices black men sometimes have.

Respectfully, I then added, "That's some gig you've got supplying the girls with pallets to fuel their fires."

It was as though he had been waiting to talk for some time because with great gusto he bragged that he charged the girls ten dollars a load of pallets, and since there were several of these rapidly burning bonfires going all-night, business was brisk and very profitable. He also made money from the resale of the items he bought for the girls at the bodega. And his eyes glistened as he stated, "I don't allow no competitors."

He asked me if I would like to join him now for the short ride to the vacant lot where he picks-up the loads of pallets. Said he wanted to talk to me about something. I got the feeling he knew who I was, that's why he had confidence in me, but that he was not one to bring it up if I didn't. But as I stepped into the passenger seat I had no idea what he wanted to talk to me about.

Right after he revved up the old station wagon's engine, I found out. He told me that in about a month he was going down to South Carolina for two weeks and wanted me to "consider filling-in" for him for that period.

"I'll need to think about it," I replied, honestly.

"You keep everything you make," he said slowly, to underscore the absence of kickback. "Two-hundred clear, a night. Nice and easy. Plus free sex."

Sex?! I thought to myself. What the fuck's he talking about? He must mean with one of the few real girls. Or, a long term ex-con, which he likely was, probably fucks them all in the ass. No way, I assured myself, was he implying that I am one of those who enjoys the COMPLETE versatility a chick with a dick has to offer.

"I dig a blow-job from just about any of these whores—which I sometimes accept in lieu of fare—but that's as far as it goes," I said.

"Whatever . . ." he replied, offhandedly.

If he had not replied, the issue would have been closed. "Whatever" did not close it for me. "You know man," I said, "I came up in the Meatpacking District, 16th on the far West Side, lots of wild shit. A few of us teenage boys would get blow-jobs from a tall, lean, neighborhood Cuban chick with a dick, who'd socialize with passing friends and neighbors from out her ground floor window. She was a prostitute, but would do certain teenage boys she dug on for free. Her name was Perfecta. I was sixteen. Never paid.

"So," I continue, speeding up my delivery to get to the point, "it's just me and her, on a hot summer's night, in her apartment. Stopped by hoping for a quick blow-job on the way home after a whole day of stocking the dairy aisle at Daitch Shopwell. Perfecta poured us each a rum and Coke. I think she spiked mine, because I passed out right on her bed...

"I was awakened to a feeling of something hard pressing up against my bare ass. Perfecta had pulled down my pants and rolled me over and was trying to fuck ME in the ass! Turned quickly onto to my back and slugged the naked Perfecta square in the face with my right fist—knocking her off the bed onto the floor, and drawing blood.

"'Motherfucker!' she screamed, rising unsteadily to her feet. 'You take blood from my face, now I keel you!' Pulling up my pants, I'm running out of her apartment, with her—after very quickly grabbing herself a weapon from the kitchen—chasing me out into the street."

At this point, we arrive on the lot. Kent asks me to keep on with my story. Which was good, because I had no intention of stopping—

"We're squared off in the street. Me, bare-chested and pants opened at the waist, and this titted, tall Perfecta with her considerable dick—NAKED—ready to bash my head in with a steel bar. Well, I remember feeling relieved that it wasn't a machete she had—because on the street I don't run.

"A girl who'd been sitting on her front stoop smoking and saw it all go down, would later tell me that everybody hanging outside very quickly crowded around this freaky face-off and was going fucking crazy. I have no memory of that, because I was completely locked in on the armed Perfecta—

"'Motherfucker, I keel you!' shouted the bloody faced Perfecta, swinging the bar at my head. I pulled back to dodge the blow, and when the bar slowed down as it finished its arc, I stepped in and snatched it away with my right hand. Held it like a spear and chased her ten or so yards as she fled back into her apartment. Everyone knew I could have caught up and destroyed her, but chose not to. I did knock out her front window with the end of the bar and chucked it back into her apartment. Then I heard sirens. Ran home."

"Funny shit," said Kent, nodding approval.

"It ain't quite over."

"Say what?" said Kent, surprised.

"Well, the next day I'm told by a buddy of mine that I'd better watch my back, because supposedly Perfecta had taken out a contract on me. For the next few weeks, I had to keep looking over my shoulder. It was a drag. So I bought a bottle of Cuba Libre Rum for her, and through this same buddy arranged for a peace meeting. On my way over to her place I also bought a liter of ice-cold Coke. She blew me."

Wordlessly, we now exited his station wagon.

There were hundreds of dumped pallets in the lot. I helped him load and we headed to a dying bonfire surrounded by the girls. As soon as we pulled up and got out, a regular, red-headed, black chick, flashing bare skinny legs, in hot pink hot-pants and a red bikini top, approached Kent. Pointing at a wisp of a girl who stood shivering by a corner bonfire less than half a block away, she asked, in a shockingly high-pitched little voice, for permission to "cut that high yaller little bitch who dissed me."

"OK," replied Kent, without any inquiry. "But don't cut her so she can't work!"

As Kent sent the load of pallets crashing onto the sidewalk, I observed two six-foot-plus chicks with dicks sharing a laugh. One caught me eyeing them and blew me a kiss. Unlike the regular girls, they need no man to provide them with protection. If provoked, they would, without any hesitation, shred your face with a razor that they kept stashed on their person, easily accessible. Inexplicably, a warm flash of affinity with these chicks with dicks passed through me. I got scared. And I don't get scared.

Kent pocketed his payment, and we got back into his station wagon. I wasted no time. "Kent," I said, "I appreciate your offer to fill-in for you but I can't commit to it".

"Hey man, absolutely YOU do not get involved in any shit between the bitches."

I said it as it hit me, "If a chick can have a dick, then a fighter can change his ID and fight in another state."

"What the fuck you talkin' about man?"

Don't Blame Me

At three-thirty on the sixteenth of September the first of two open to the public (free) Yom Kippur 5763 Yizkor services at Temple Beth Torah would begin. And, stated the recorded phone announcement, to ensure entry it's advised you arrive (to wait in line outside the temple) half an hour before.

From past experience, I knew, that at three-twenty-five (five minutes before starting time) entry tickets would be distributed to the first two-hundred-eight people in line. If you were not among this first group of entrants you'd have to remain in line another hour for the second and final free service (tentatively scheduled for four-thirty) to begin. This arrangement eventually accommodated all of the close to four-hundred worshippers who'd show up on this holiest of all Jewish holidays for the free Yizkor service, which memorialized closely related dearly departed.

Since age fourteen, twenty-nine years ago, I may have missed one year due to an eight-thousand-pound depression. Otherwise, every year, in honor of my beloved mother I'd make it my business to attend a Yizkor service on Yom Kippur.

To make sure I'd gain admission to the three-thirty service, I arrived two-thirty, a full hour early. About fifty people were already in line, on the Second Avenue side of Temple Beth Torah, when I took my place this sunny, very warm afternoon on the Upper East Side of Manhattan. Jacket already off, I loosened my tie and unbuttoned the top button of my shirt, feeling fortunate to be situated under the shade of a small tree. Resigned to stand and wait an hour, alone, I'd let time pass, alternately observing the stream of passersby and the gabby line gatherings to the front and rear of me. The gabby line gatherings proved to be far more interesting.

Directly before me stood a threesome consisting of a short, sturdy old man in a peaked cap, a frumpy, fifty-something woman, and a pushing-thirty version of the frump. The old man impressed me. Although he had a hearing-aid in each ear and that fossilized look of the truly old, he stood erect and looked pain free. He had to be well into his eighties. And that burnt me because it brought to mind that for the past month, summoned down to Bonita Springs Florida, grinding herself into dust attending to the needs of her helpless, hospitalized, stroke-stricken, seventy-year-old mother, was the woman I love.

Behind me, was an instantly forgettable couple. Never would they need to don masks if they paired as bandits.

In a gabby gathering just ahead of the threesome before me, I spotted the sensational cream-colored face of a young blond woman. Dreamy, fragile, and ready. Like a Sixties Marianne Faithful. I could always stare at *her*. That this young woman, attired appropriately for the occasion in a modest brown shirtdress, had the torso of a tree stump did not have to come into play—

"I'm not even going in," shrilled a male voice into the back of my head, "and I'm pissed at this friggin' system." Turned around, it was Mr. Instantly Forgettable into his cell phone.

"That's why you're pissed!" I blurted at him. And turned back around. What a putz. The temple is providing a perfectly good service in an organized manner to non-members, and the system is no good? Like he, Mr. Instantly Forgettable, could come up with a better system. Better for who? Him. And what the fuck's he doing waiting in line if he's not going in. Keeping his female counterpart company, I guess. If you're going to do that just keep your trap shut and do it. And who could be on the other end of a call like that? His mother?

The frump was now addressing the frumpette, "You should have asked them to get up." The frumpette, it seems, had accompanied the old man up to the three reserved—for the elderly and infirm—benches by the entrance, but all seats were taken. "But he," responded the frumpette, head gesturing at the old man, "said not to. That it was okay."

I'll gladly get one of those thoughtless cows to get up, I felt like interjecting. But figured it's not my business to overrule what the old man had told the frumpette. Anyway, the sturdy old man, jacket in hand, now walked away with the frumpette. Leaving the frump to hold their place in line. I told the frump I'd hold their place if she wanted to join them. No thanks, said the frump. Who went on to inform that the frumpette was her daughter. And the old man, her father. He was up visiting from his suburban Philadelphia home. Ninety-six years old, he retired from his career as gym teacher at seventy-three. A widower, he refused to move to a retirement community. Her only concern was his driving. And being that he lived in the suburbs he had to drive some. *Ninety-six.*

"God bless him," I officiously pronounced, and shifted my sights beyond her to Marianne Faithful Face. She was chatting with a taller, bare shouldered, collagen-lipped brunette. They faced a wavy-brown-haired, squat man, his back, for the most part, to me. In a navy blue suit, he stood at ease between the two. Closer to Marianne Faithful Face. Husband, brother, or chiropractor. Very possibly, two of three. When the conversation appeared to shift away from her, the brunette began licking around her enhanced lips. Deflation anxiety? Twice around with tongue, before doing an about face to feature her—thanks to tight black stylish pants—anti-gravity butt. More man-hunter than mourner, for this somber service a burka, in my opinion, would've been more appropriate attire.

Speaking of burkas, the entire curb was blocked off by four-feet-high cement barricades to prevent against the possibility of Jew-hating terrorists crashing an explosives-loaded van into the temple. Four formidable plain-clothes (jacket and tie) clad security guards were privately hired to work the event. Retired cops. Two were stationed in the entrance. And two worked the avenue. Alongside a bus stop, about twenty feet up ahead of me, I noticed the frumpette and the old man sitting atop the ass accommodative flat surface of the cement barricade. Beneath a pitiless sun, leisurely they chatted, as city busses rolled up and away bathing the twosome in the most noxious fumes the city has to offer. With certainty, I'd wager, that one hit of that bus exhaust is worse for your health than 30,000 years of second-hand cigarette smoke. And I loathe cigarette smoke. Ninety-six-years-old and he couldn't care less. *Damn*. I'd have to go back to my teenage years to sit unbothered in what was an open air gas chamber. Not being overly concerned about things had to be the longevity key.

"Look at him sitting there," I excitedly urged the frump, pointing at him after tapping her shoulder, "he's like a teenager!" And hoped, immediately after saying it, that I didn't curse him with the evil eye. The frump smiled. I'd have felt a lot better if she'd have *pooh, pooh, poohed* at him (it had to be three times), like my mother (who was from a small dirt poor shtetl in Poland) would on me, following it with *kenna hora*[*] if someone tossed a flattering comment my way.

Not only does this double talisman not hurt, I daresay it is vital. This is because, very commonly, unconscious human envy is hidden beneath words of good will. Left unchecked in the air these words are live negative energy. This negative energy often can survive just long enough (a matter of seconds) to infiltrate one of the eternally wavering, otherwise impotent, air rampant, deathly spirits that witness us. Symbiotically merged, this force of misfortune slips simply into the soul of the accursed. As simply as the spirit slips from the body when one gives up the ghost. Anyway, I got good and lost. . . after forcibly carrying off Ms. Marianne Faithful Face and her ass offering associate. . . .

Snapped to when one of the plain clothed security guards said—excuse me sir—to me and handed me a ticket for entry. The two women had apparently been in my depraved custody for close to forty minutes!

---

* Yiddish - *may the evil eye stay away*

In back of me, a shrill male voice complained about "this system." It was, of course, Mr. Instantly Forgettable. Complaining to Mr. Ticket Distributor, who was in the process of handing him an admission ticket. Mr. Ticket Distributor completely ignored the words of Mr. Instantly Forgettable. He was a genius.

Within two minutes the line started to move. The frumpette and her grandfather returned. As though I mattered not, a robust gray couple waving their tickets cut right in front of me. I let it slide because they were senior citizens. And, more importantly, because I needed to adjust into a prayerful mindset—

"I'm a Jewish person! You can't do this!! I'm a Jewish person!" Came the yells from the entrance. The two women doing the yelling were being blocked from entering the temple by a security guard. Apparently, this ticketless twosome had shamelessly rushed the entrance. Middle-aged, layered in make-up, and sporting fresh bouffant hairdos, I could sense these weren't merely East Village-chic invaders out for an afternoon frolic, or simply result-oriented yenta perpetrators, but the real deal—the unconquerably insane. From my long years in the Bronx, I knew the type very well. They are the handful of white people left in certain Bronx neighborhoods (Pelham Parkway for one), not counting the influx of Albanians, Russians, and other assorted East European immigrants who appeared during the nineties. All day, they hang-out in Burger King loudly swapping stories of their imagined rendezvous with movie stars, while easily digesting Whoppers chased with coffee. Nighttime often brings about a shift in venue to a rowdy bingo parlor for an evening of gaming or an otherwise empty dump of a diner for extended hours of very minimal ordering and plenty of harmless delusional conversation. What drew this duo—never before seen in the area—to Temple Beth Torah this Yom Kippur? Who knows? Maybe they were looking for me. They do enjoy a good outing. Anyway, a gentleman on scene at the face-off, who must've been and an elected officer of the temple, intervened, advising the security guards to allow the two ticketless line-busting sisters of screwiness to enter. Terrorists, they weren't. Like the security guard who completely ignored Mr. Instantly Forgettable, he was a genius.

The line then moved smoothly. And as was the case with all in line who preceded me, when I reached the front I had to stop momentarily in order for a security guard to perfunctorily wave a metal-detecting wand down away from my body before being permitted to enter the temple.

The vast makeshift room of worship was filled with rows and rows of pre-arranged folding chairs. One of the first fifty or so entrants,

I pounced upon an empty aisle seat closest to the exit. In another part of the temple was the main room, which was where services for members (payers of a considerable annual fee) were held. That room had cushioned benches and stained glass windows. Which is not to say that there was anything wrong with the well air-conditioned makeshift room. Up front, we had a podium. Several feet to its left and slightly to its rear was an ark containing two torahs. The room filled fast. Not much jockeying around. Within a couple minutes, few seats remained available. Looking around, I realized that the two sisters of screwiness were not yet in the room. They must have gone straight to the ladies room for extensive powdering. *Fuck*, one of the few empty seats is to my immediate right, practically in my lap. One of them will probably come in and sit there! Her crazy vibes destroying my prayerful mood. And in they marched—past me—to the other side of the room. Where they had to sit apart, but could at least be in the same section. If either would've taken the seat next to me I'd surely have retreated to the back of the room and stood for the entire service. With warm welcoming eyes, I greeted the old woman who came in and sat down next to me.

A reform synagogue, the men did don yarmulkes but the cantor was a young woman (and not bad-looking). She sang the King James version of Psalm 23 sweetly, *The Lord is my shepherd*...As soon as she finished, the carefully coiffed, pleasantly plump, youthful-looking rabbi calmly adjusted his tallis, before launching into a pat and flat spiel about some former classmate of his named Davidoff...Cancer...Not pausing, as chairs shuffled and chatter broke out on the other side of the room. I had not expected the two sisters of screwiness to act up during the service, and when I looked over to the other side of the room I spotted each of them seated apart quietly. From my vantage point, there was no discernible pocket of ruckus. The disturbance ceased as quickly as it started. Not missing a monotonous beat, on spoke the rabbi...Stopping not, a few minutes later, when, in through the door burst a couple of beefy EMS men going directly past him to the renewed shuffling and buzzing coming from the other side of the room.

Toward the rear, in the far aisle of that side of the immense room, I recognized the frump and frumpette standing among six or seven loosely huddled people. Collectively, the group took on the form of a protoplasm. In the middle of a row close to the protoplasm, the two EMS men eclipsed the seated person to whom they were attending. A minute later (the rabbi was plodding on about Davidoff's brave battle), the protoplasm split, allowing the EMS men to walk the dwarfed and bewildered, white tee-shirted, ninety-six-year-old, frump/frumpette progenitor through. At both sides the old gentleman was supported by an EMS man gripping him beneath each armpit as they continued on, slowly stepping several steady paces up the aisle, before he collapsed slack into their strength. Totally self-absorbed, the rabbi took a breath (having buried Davidoff, he somehow was not yet finished) when, coincidentally, directly past him en route out, the old man was carried. One EMS worker gripped him under his armpits and the other by his ankles. The body sagged like a hammock beneath the weight of a slumbering suburbanite. Sheepishly, the frump—*she'd volunteered his age, I'd NEVER have asked*—and frumpette followed. The rabbi reacted to the glum procession before him with a momentary look of blank indifference, before droning on with his speech. A minute or two later, he wrapped up. And I—*I swear*—when I told the frump her aged father displayed the physical ease of a teenager, I wished *not* to curse him.

Ballad of Caleb Belleu

He was ready to give her a goodnight kiss and be on his way, when she invited him in. Right after their first date, a movie, "American Graffiti," up on Fordham Road at the Capri. The Bronx, in April of seventy-three.

He, was Caleb Belleu. An intensely guarded, directionless 18-year-old. And, his nubile brunette date was 17-year-old Shelly Gold. Her house was exactly eight blocks and a park from "the schoolyard" of P.S. 89. Where he hung out, among a dangling bunch of drug wrangling girl conquerors.

Shelly loved the movie and loved him. Why not, Caleb was a naturally-muscled pretty boy who exuded an attractive aura of melancholia. He also was deceptively bright and very respectful. His godmother said he looked like the actor Montgomery Clift.

What he didn't have was a J-O-B. A high school graduate, at times, he talked of college. But talk was all it was.

He'd forgotten the movie as soon as it ended. It was unreal to him. But on the bus ride back to their neighborhood, he told Shelly, he "also, liked the movie a lot."

He did like her. Besides being good-looking and crazy about him, she was smart and smiled freely. A senior in high school, she got good grades. Shelly did not hang out. She was unknown to the guys he hung with.

He had seen her on Allerton Avenue a couple of times, alone, shopping. This afternoon, when he spotted her across the street, he forced himself to approach her. And as his heart tried to pound out of his head, he struck up a conversation. The interest was unmistakably mutual and their "eight—tonight" date set.

That she was unknown to the guys he hung with was of paramount importance to Caleb. He would not have to be a master of eroticism. There was no risk of exposure.

You see, Caleb was a virgin. He was very ashamed of it. He had more than his share of opportunities to change that, but was afraid that word of his virginity would get out. Or, worse yet, he'd fuck up—fucking.

Caleb was born, a bastard, to a loving mother who doted heavily on her sparkling boy. When the child asked about his father she'd say, "I'll let you know the whole story, when you are old enough to understand." An otherwise healthy young woman, she suffered from asthma.

The boy loved his mother very much, but by the time he reached puberty he wished she'd JUST leave him alone. He began breaking away.

The night Caleb was out at his first ever petting party his mother DIED during an asthma attack. He never cried. At the party, shy 13-year-old Caleb had been an intimidated observer. At 18, the shy young man remained—an intimidated observer.

His mother had begged him to stay home that night. But then, she always wanted only him. If only he listened and stayed home that night she . . .

His widowed godmother took him right in, to her two-room housing-projects apartment. Infirm and elderly, she was glad to have him around. They lived off her social security check.

The young man still lived there with her. The cramped apartment was similar to the one he had lived in with his mother, in the adjacent building.

Shelly led Caleb up the carpeted staircase of her sleeping family's upholstered home. Self-conscious, to the point of paranoia, Caleb assured himself that the transformation he was feeling, inwardly, into a grotesque space alien trespasser could not be real and continued to follow Shelly's weakest asset on its ascension to the second floor.

Shelly's room was a soft pink. Shelly was red hot for the blue boy—Caleb. As the blue boy stood, ruminating on how wondrously shiny the doorknob of her closet door was—she jumped him.

Healthy and inexperienced, she had decided it would be Caleb, and it would be now. Apparently, she wasn't concerned about her parents. He surely couldn't be. After all, he was a FUCKIN' MAN, wasn't he?

He had to piss and he pushed her off and excused himself. She told him to tiptoe through the hall to the next door on the left for the toilet. He did. He was extremely uptight. He couldn't piss. He threatened himself with death by violence.

It didn't help.

When he got back to the pink room the hot girl AGAIN jumped him. They groped, kissed, and grinded. The pressure from his bladder was becoming painful. His manhood—flaccid. Caleb excused himself again.

And again, couldn't piss.

He tiptoed back to Shelly's room, cursed with uneasiness concerning her sleeping parents, unowned performance anxiety, and painful pressure from his bladder. She now wanted to put "it" into her mouth. He dropped his jeans to his knees. Had to. She dropped to her knees and put it into her mouth. It had no reaction to her oral action.

"Shel-lee," the phlegmy call of her mother coincided with the flick of the light switch from the toilet. Instantly, Caleb pulled—up—his jeans and Shelly—down—her blouse—rumpled—they sat—apart—on her bed.

"Shel-lee are you o-kay?"

"Yes, mom."

"Did you have a good time?"

Smiling into Caleb's grimace Shelly quickly took his hand and kissed it. She then replied to her mother, "Yes mom."

"Shelly, next time your father and I want to meet Cu-pid."

"Okay, and it's Ca-leb mom, Ca-leb, not Cupid."

"So long as he's white. Goodnight baby."

"Goodnight mom."

When he felt sure that her mother was back in bed he excused himself for the final time, before tiptoeing downstairs and slipping out the front door and Shelly's life, forever.

Ballooned bladder ready to burst Caleb scurried around the corner, stopped, by a blue VW Beetle, unzipped and took his dick out.

Thirty seconds would pass, a second at a time, before he could piss—fire—onto the driver-side door of the Bug.

The piss lasted four full minutes.

Piss rivulets streamed smokily fierce on the black tarred street. The Bug was drowned.

Bladder relieved but sore, Caleb lit a True Blue and took a long sucking drag on its air-filter. Exhaled, and was overcome by an avalanche of emotional inadequacy.

He couldn't piss, he didn't fuck. He was a piece of fuckin' shit.

He needed to get high. Drained of life he bleached white from rageful shame. He began the long thirteen block walk to Bill and Ray's Bar on White Plains Road, where he hoped there'd be drugs to cop.

Midway through his journey Caleb's mood blackened to a depth lower than any he had ever known. One from which, he feared, there would be no return. He walked faster.

It didn't help.

At ten past midnight Caleb arrived at the bar. His dope connection was not there. Caleb badly wanted to snort some dope, but had to settle for three bootleg Tuinals.

Immediately, he split for the bodega on the corner, bought a can of Coke and washed the boots down.

He couldn't face anyone and started aimlessly walking westward, waiting for the boots to kick-in. Three should loosen his speech slurred but leave him fairly functional mechanically. The boots did not disappoint.

Ten minutes later the pilly meltdown of Caleb's hurtin' brain began. The recklessness of the goof-ball head met his already dark agitation. This coupling made Caleb feel like "doing something."

The XXX Globe movie theater was right across the street. He crossed over. Last week a few of the guys dropped acid and went to the Globe to see "The Devil In Miss Jones."

Caleb didn't go. He would never drop acid. He felt certain he'd have a bad trip. As for the movie, to Caleb, watching XXX movies was like watching surgery.

He kept both, his aversion to XXX movies and acid abstinence to himself. He never risked ridicule.

By the Globe, he closely inspected a poster depicting a spread-eagle "Miss Jones," when he felt a hand tapping him gently on the left shoulder.

It was a kid around Caleb's age and height. But blond, chinless, and slight. A complete unknown, "Hi, I'm Peter."

Caleb knew he was being hit on, "Tsup?" he curtly questioned.

Peter stepped back and took a chance, "Do you want to go for a walk?"

"Let's go to the park." Tight and wired Caleb surprised even himself with that reply.

As they walked, less than a block to the park, Peter said, "You're the best looking guy I've ever been with."

Caleb smoked and said nothing.

The park was empty. But, that could change without hardly any notice. Peter dropped to his knees before Caleb, and Caleb dropped his jeans to his knees. Caleb gave up thinking. The night was still and warm. More like summer than spring.

Peter blew better than the whores Caleb had previously gotten blown by. His tongue was loving. Caleb felt manly and defiant. He WAS a man. So much a man, another man was blowing him.

Caleb spurted lightning into Peter's mouth. Satisfied. Caleb WAS a man.

He looked down and suddenly stepped back, sickened. Peter was jerking off. The kid had a real big dick and was releasing mightily. Disgusted, Caleb half-heartedly kicked Peter once in the chest, knocking him on his back. Pulled up his jeans and split.

Caleb knew he wasn't gay and it felt good not to give a fuck. But he did give a fuck.

Temporarily diverted by the experience in the park, his soul torment again howled bloody. Caleb began to hyperventilate. But, quickly managed to get it under control. His head needed a boost.

He got it, back at the bar, in three quick shots of Jack Daniel's. And still had close to fifty dollars on him from a three day job, helping his neighbor, Junior, distribute circulars for a new car wash up in Yonkers. He did not want to run into anyone. Left the bartender a buck tip and split across the street.

There, he hung in front of the busy newsstand and smoked. It was 1:10, but it was Saturday night. Caleb watched as cars pulled-up and were left double-parked in a line, engines still humming as drivers jumped out to pick up Sunday's papers. Obliviousness was settling on him and he gave in to it.

His oblivion was a spacey sort of reminiscence that took him—into the bus coming back from the movie sitting next to Shelly.

Before him was the sun-reddened bald crown of the gentleman's head who was seated directly in front of him.

The ears of the head would—HE—grab and like a beast gone berserk bite down on the baldness and bite and bite . . .

The thought amused him then, and broke him up now. Laughing, he took a few steps toward a—left running—brown Ford Pinto. Stopped laughing, jumped in and drove off!

The car was needed to pick up a hooker from the West Farms streets. Had to FUCK tonight! He had balked, in the past, when it came to fucking a hooker, because he figured that was like putting it into a sewer. He would NOT think that. He also resolved to be cautious with the car, but NOT to think about getting caught.

A guy he knew who could sometimes borrow an uncle's car had recently given Caleb a nighttime tour of West Farms. Like locusts, the hookers had swarmed, blanketing some blocks entirely.

Caleb took a circuitous route, using side streets to get to West Farms. He didn't even turn on the radio. He would fuck and take the subway back. He did turn on the AC. He loved AC. This was going to go right. He didn't give a fuck. It WAS right. The night would become a fond FUCKING memory.

Caleb detoured past the high-profile main strip on Tremont, where he knew hundreds of tough, hardened hookers occupied the prime street real estate.

He cruised a side street in search of an attractive part-time amateur. Once around. That was the plan. No block, would he cruise, more than once.

Immediately, he came upon a small gathering of girls hanging for business. One girl stepped toward him in his stopped Pinto. He waved her off and signaled for one from the rear. Bingo.

Long limbed for a small girl—Venus—was slim yet very shapely. She had dark brown skin, full red lips, and a short afro haircut. Caleb found her very attractive.

He would be her first trick of the night. Perfect, he thought, she's fresh. Not yet fouled.

Twenty bucks to fuck and ten more for the hour at the Royal Ostrich Motel.

Done.

Caleb put the Pinto into drive and headed, the couple blocks, to Southern Boulevard. The Royal Ostrich was a few miles north, on Southern Boulevard and 183rd.

For Caleb, Venus had made an exception. She preferred to work, cars only, at ten bucks a blow-job. But, she was taken with Caleb's movie star good looks. And even though she pinned him for being stoned, she could sense that he was no problem.

She could. She could sense if a john was trouble. If she got bad vibes she was OUT of the car.

Unfortunately for Venus, she did not incorporate this intuitive gift into her "private" life. All, her past and present boyfriends were trouble.

She asked Caleb for a cigarette. He dug her saucy little voice and noticed that the green miniskirt and platform shoes she wore did not age her fresh schoolgirl face. He handed her a cigarette. She had a lighter. Venus lit up and smoked.

Feeling good, Caleb asked her, "Do you go to school?"

Venus replied that she had gone to all girls Walton High for two years, before dropping out, "because the school was bugged-out, wild, all bull-dyke bitches." Caleb had heard that about Walton.

She then proudly proclaimed, "I passed the Bronx High School of Science exam."

"So, why didn't you go?"

"I wouldn't have known anyone there, so I asked my father what he thought."

"What he say?"

"He said, 'You have a nice little shape—you'll do fine.'"

Caleb had no response to that, and cruised on through a row of green lights on Southern Boulevard. Venus commented on how good the AC felt.

A rush of love flushsuddened Caleb. He considered running away with her.

Fuck everybody.

At a red light, a McDonald's was on their right. Caleb asked Venus if she wanted to stop for something to eat.

"Maybe," she purred, "after."

In less than two minutes they'd reach the Royal Ostrich, and her reply pleased Caleb.

The light turned green, and as his right foot shifted and pressed gently down on the gas, he laughed to himself, wondering how anyone could come up with a name for a motel as ridiculous as—

"Oh fu-uck!" shrieked Venus, blasting his thought process. A shrill siren mixed hellish with her shriek.

Up in the rear-view mirror Caleb saw a police car flashing him over. Caleb, numbly, pulled over. Bolting from the car, Venus took to flight—

The lone cop leapt out of his car, revolver cocked and drawn— pointed down—by his right thigh.

"Hold it right there!" he shouted at the fleeing girl's back. She kept running. The revolver remained—pointed down—by his right thigh.

Out of his body, mind, and car—it was Caleb—rushing the cop, "She had nothing to—"

The first bullet blew through his arm—another—into his heart. Downed Caleb. Out a tenement window a female voice flew, "Cop shot da keed—dead!" Traffic stopped. Salsa and sirens.

The puddles were red.

Uptown Express

The connecting door in the back of the car clack-bangs open. And an expressionless Asian man, covered like a Christmas tree, with assorted junk, such as glow-in-the-dark yo-yos and ringing kiddy cellphones emerges. To trumpet his presence, he shakes a brain-banging rattle. And advances cautiously through strap-hanging passengers. Amid whom, I stand.

As he passes I'm tempted to stop him, to tell him how that blood-curdling rattle is exactly what I've been searching for, for the greater part of my adult life. But I restrain myself, realizing he's just another man, like myself, doing what he needs to survive.

A walkman wired kid maintains his pigeon head bop while gesturing to the man for batteries.

Eighty-Sixth and Lex., Manhattan's Upper East Side, is next. It's the stop before Harlem on this Bronx bound number 5 subway. Uptown Express.

It is at this Eighty-Sixth Street stop that I can always assure myself of my psychic powers. I merely will the command, and every white person in the car pours out. Tonight is no different.

At times, I've been tempted to shout that command, "All white fuckers off!" But I'm adjusted too well, or I'm too tightly adjusted. Depends on how you look at it.

The last white man—I am—and maneuver to a mid-car seat vacated by a trim yuppie girl with horsy good looks and a smart black leather briefcase.

It's 8:00 p.m., and only a few people need to stand.

After scanning all for psychotic vibes and untreatable tuberculosis, I deem it safe to shut my tired eyes for the few minutes between stops. Unless, I hear the quick crescendo clack of a connecting door sliding open.

I need to see who gets on at each stop and who enters from between cars.

Surprises, no.

Eyes shut I space, for what could very well be a personal best ten minutes straight, before the train screeches a metallic bone chill into the Harlem station. Where, we come to a jerking halt. More people exit than enter.

Subsequent stops are up the Bronx and local. Frequent and numerous. Eyes open.

A restless teenage boy passes quickly through the length of the car into another and then probably into another.

The empty orange can of Sunkist orange soda rolling on the floor stops by me.

I shove it aside with my foot and looking downward am reminded of the bruised condition of the knuckles on my right hand. On my lap rest my hands.

How the fuck do you bloody your knuckles punching a wall—when you're asleep?

Three stops—in ten minutes—later, we emerge from the bleak tunnel into the night light, high on the el, pulling into Jackson Avenue.

I kick the bruised knuckles out of my head.

At Jackson, the doors to the platform and the connecting door on my far left bang open in unison.

I take a couple seconds to see who's coming and going before looking left, to the back end of the car, where stands a five-feet-tall troll with chest-length, bushy, charcoal-colored hair.

The troll, a female, holds a long red umbrella. Mutters incoherent Spanish and attempts—without warning—to thrust the point of the long umbrella through the forehead of a seated lady, over whom, she stands. Umbrella bayonet.

The seated black lady raises a forearm and blocks the shockingly out-of-the-blue but sluggish attack. Ashen, she sits frozen.

Gripping the umbrella with both hands, like a bayonet, the huntress faces the rest of the car, lengthwise. Outside of yours truly there are only a few others in the car. An old lady seated opposite me, and a couple down the other end absorbed in conversation. The old lady stares at me. I stare at the troll.

As the seemingly wind-blown dark cloud that is troll approaches I swallow the air psychotic.

I remove my wallet from my back right pocket. Over me, the troll now stands. Umbrella alert, I fix a menacing—don't MAKE ME do my duty—glare on the troll and flash my blue Chase Master Card at her—

Terrified, the troll flees into the car up ahead, pausing momentarily, to poke the orange soda can with the tip of her long red umbrella bayonet.

Sighing deep relief, the old lady seated across from me launches into non-stop Spanish at her new best friend—me. She needs to, to expel her troll induced remnant terror. I understand, but I do not understand much Spanish.

Three stops later, at Simpson, she's still at it. And I continue to automatically nod respectful acknowledgment. Although, I'm no longer really listening. When I was listening, I was able to pick up on her strong feelings about two things. One, her desire to retire to Puerto Rico. And two, her dislike of Dominicans.

In the shelter of her forceful chatter, I space. . . .

At East Tremont the old lady rises to exit. In five or so more minutes I'll be getting off. She exits after we exchange good wishes. On rolls the train.

I spot the woman who was attacked by the troll now sitting in the front-end corner of the car. I did not see her move. If the troll returns it will be through that connecting front-door.

I stand, zip my jacket, and walk to the front. There, strap-hanging left-handed, I lean back on the door from which I'll exit. Kill minutes here.

Glance down at my bruised knuckles and it becomes clear. Dream life reflects the human experience. The human experience must be the reflection of yet another dream. The wall had it coming.

Take the few steps over to the woman whom the troll attacked. Tell her I'm real glad she didn't get hurt.

"Bitch comes back I'll light her hair on fire!"

I nod approvingly. That explains the yellow Bic lighter wrapped in her right fist.

The conductor calls, "Morris Park!" Me.

Skip over the gap onto the platform soon as the doors slide open. Into the night. Under a blank sky.

Things Equal to Things Equal Things

After flushing the toilet and washing his hands, O., feeling buoyant and hungry, stepped through the closet-sized foyer, back into the dinette. Before, he had been constipated and hungry.

On the small circular oak dining table was his Chinese take-out meal of beef with orange flavor. A spicy combination of sliced tender beef sautéed in hot pepper sauce with mandarin orange peel flavor, his favorite. Well-salaried (he was an actuary), the reserved, trim and fit, graying bachelor, easily afforded his three room mid-town Manhattan rental and all his meals out. He never cooked. He'd already carefully transferred the food from the cardboard containers into two ceramic dishes—so that it would taste better.

Cold air blew into the room. O. ALWAYS opened the window when he arrived home. He'd replace the old screen that fell out, down five stories into the back alley, tomorrow. He needed air—even in the winter. A motionless pigeon, its back to O., had parked on the window-sill.

"OOGA—BOOGA—FUCKYA—AAAAGH!" war-cried O.—flailing his arms as he mocked a rush at the black pigeon. The pigeon was not instantly alarmed, but, after a moment, flew off. Tickled by his ability to erupt into tongues, the savage tribal warrior sat down to feast.

Funny, he thought to himself, I've been here three years and there has never been a pigeon by my window. Just sparrows. O. forked up a bite-size piece of translucent orange goo soaked beef, and noticed a small dent in the bed of white rice. Two chews, and swallowed the beef. DELICIOUS!

He turned his head left to face the window for a fresh hit of direct cold air and was reminded of the filthy rat with wings, before turning back to his meal and the dent in the white bed of rice. The room darkened before his very eyes. The possibility was screenless. The feathered rat had flown in and peck-dented the rice! It COULD'VE happened. He had failed to protect himself! It happened. He'd come to expect the worst. The rice was bad! But, he had caught it in time. He'd eat the beef. He'd toss the rice—and forget it!

Robbed at gunpoint last year, O. did not at all panic. But, germ torpedoes snowballed invisible. The pigeon had SAT in the rice! How else could you explain such a dent? It was the sweet savory beef that had been pecked—He was ALREADY poisoned!

As YOU would—if a fire were to ignite beneath your seated bottom—O. reflexively sprang from his chair—and shut the sliding window down. Desperate as a cornered rabbit fighting for its very survival, he grabbed both plates (one in each hand), heavy-footed two steps to the small olive-colored plastic garbage receptacle, dumped the food and put the dishes into the sink.

In the bathroom, he now scrubbed his hands before splashing cool water on his sweaty face. Relieved, he was nonetheless plunged up to his neck in self-hate muck. He approached the kitchen sink tentatively.

With a sopping sudsy sponge he washed the dishes in warm water, and was wiping a dinner plate dry with a dish towel—when he was overcome by the realization of his own stupidity. Hot water! He'd HAVE TO repeat the procedure. But this time, he'd think it through in advance.

The pigeon contaminated the food. The food contaminated the plates. The pigeon contaminated the plates. Simple logic. If A=B and B=C then A=C. Things equal to things equal things. An axiom. The pigeon contaminated the food contaminated the plates contaminated the sponge contaminated the dish towel—

The dish towel—here, the hot water application theory hit a snag. The plates and sponge were readily redeemable. If he hand washed the dish towel it would have to be hung to dry. It went into the hamper. After quickly washing his hands with soap and water, he stepped from the bathroom to grab a dish towel from the top shelf of the foyer closet. And then, re-entered the kitchen. Taking no chances, he did not hang the fresh dish towel on the hook over the sink, whereupon the contaminated towel had hung.

His hands were dry and itchy from overexposure to water. So, from a bottom cabinet, he withdrew a pair of yellow rubber gloves. Gloved, O. washed the two dishes and lone fork in hot water with the sopping sudsy sponge. His hands felt clammy and suffocated in the rubber gloves. THE SAME GLOVES HE'D USED TO WASH THE BATHROOM FLOOR THREE WEEKS AGO?! If he were a pinball machine T-I-L-T would've emblazoned his forehead as he blew from his apartment into the hallway carrying the two dishes, fork and sponge, and tossed them down the compactor chute.

Momentarily relieved, in his apartment, he made a mental note that tomorrow he'd HAVE TO replace the sponge and plates, at lunch break or after work. It was too late now, stores were closed. And the rubber gloves, wet, on the floor of the kitchen WET kitchen FLOOR!— ARM INTO CLOSET FOR PARKA—O. fled torturous iron mind spiral reality—

In the street, on he walked, downtown...Stopping, in the East Village, to wolf down a slice of pizza. He then headed back.

Early tomorrow, O. would awaken, face buried in his own warm scent in his pillow. Relieved, that he had not been poisoned by the one bite of savory orange beef. That he had again eluded imminent catastrophe. He'd leave for work, clean shaven and showered. His short shopping list folded neatly into an inner-compartment of his attaché case. Fantasizing, that on this day of comforting drudgery, something, something good, for him, was in the air.

Kiss of Death

Moneyed, young, and full of himself, Manhattan stockbroker Jack Barish strode home up mid-town Madison Avenue, mightily. And why not? His commission pace was well ahead of last year's personal high, he was still only thirty-one, and he was not a bad looking guy. His time had come. Reagan had the White House and Jack had the mid-western blond babes. And come, he did. A long way from his working-class Bronx roots.

As was his habit, Jack ran his right hand back through his thinning hair. Still there. This, he did, without missing a stride. He chuckled, realizing, that on a cold winter's night like this, if his mother had her way he'd still be donning a woolen stocking cap. Pulled down to keep his ears—

"Ya wanna go out?" screeched a female birdy voice, from the vestibule of a Chase Manhattan Bank a few feet from Jack, interrupting his meditative self-adulation in motion. Looking around, he was the only one. She was, indeed, addressing him.

Hookers do not hang around here, Jack thought, as he took in the Afghan coated, shadowy little figure. No way, was she a cop. "How much for up the ass?" shot mind swaggering Jack, fucking around.

"How would you like to get fucked in the ass?" she shot back.

She's got a point, thought Jack. Desperate and crazy enough to solicit him, a stranger, albeit, one clad in a Brooks Brothers cashmere overcoat, at a spot where hooking was not to be done and her asshole is non-negotiable. The maker of deals got a kick out of that.

"I'm going for something to eat," he announced. "Actually, I was going to detour over to the Oyster Bar where they know Jack Barish. But, If you'd like to have something, we can do Chinese or pizza. I'm buying."

"Okay," she replied.

From the dim vestibule, she emerged. Jack was surprised. Whatever kind of addict she was, she didn't look too bad. One or two pimples on a cute but gaunt face. About his age. Big brown eyes beneath big brown curls.

Scanning the surrounding area, up ahead on the other side of Madison by 40th Street, Jack saw a very small Chinese take-out restaurant. Highly unlikely, he decided, that anyone who mattered would walk in on them at that hole in the wall. There, they went to eat. Side by side, they stood by the counter as Jack peeled a lone ten from a roll of twenties, paying for their orders upfront. He received only loose change in return. Taking off their coats and hanging them on back of their chairs, they sat at the orange Formica table for two. Face to face. Not surprisingly, she was very thin. The three remaining tables were unoccupied. His briefcase, he positioned on the floor between his Italian loafered feet.

"How are you?" she emptily asked.

"I'm always good." replied Jack, delivering his stock go-getter.

Beneath the bright fluorescent light, however, what remained of his magnanimous dinner invitation moment, dissipated before a subtle dread yellow hue which surrounded her eyes like a somewhat irregular mask of Zorro. He simply did not want to look at her. Her mere presence rankled him. He considered asking her to sit at another table, but decided that was too cruel. He'd endure. Looking through her, he instead, launched into an anger fueled *you too can do it!* autobiographical monologue—

"I," loudly announced Jack Barish, before repeating in a low, pressed tone, "I...was the only Jewish kid on a tough block. Top it off, I sucked in school. Zero confidence. *Can you believe it...?* Thank God, though, nature took its proper course and I wound up where I belonged—on top. Had my kosher-deli counterman father ever taught me anything about anything manly, or, for that matter, anything about anything, that's the way it always would've been. But you know what? The simpleton did the best he could. No one ever said life is fair!"

"Listen," continued Jack, resting his palms flat on the table as he straightened-up fully in his chair, "the thing is, fate was very kind to me. Like the man upstairs took a personal interest in Jack Barish. And to put what I'm about to pass on to you into proper perspective, I gave you some background. No one really knows that about Jack Barish. Or, that I didn't have *anything* together until after I turned eighteen."

"So there I am, clueless and lonely, the very night before I hit eighteen, thirteen years ago, March 31,1976—to be exact. Amazing...later that night, the *two tools* needed for achieving the American Dream would be revealed to me—*All I ever really needed to know!* At the RKO Fordham, in one, chance, viewing of what turned out to be a totally awesome new movie called 'Rocky'! *Eye of the tiger!* and *Go for it!* And, I absorbed them. *Eye of the tiger!* and *Go for it! Eye of the tiger!* and *Go for it! Eye of the tiger!* and *Go for it!* Father fucked your mouth when you were in the crib? It don't mean shit! Reach for a tool! Reach for a tool! I don't know why I'm even trying to help you."

Two trays of food were then set before them by the hustling counterman.

Unaffected by Jack's lecture, before either of them raised a plastic fork, she asked, "Would you please buy me a Brandy Alexander?"

The timing and outlandishness of this request caused Jack to echo, incredulously, "A Brandy Alexander?" noticing, for the first time, that her big brown eyes moved in concert with each other but seemed to float around unconnected to any other aspect of her being. And it shook his yuppie ass, more than he thought it should—

"Yeah," she snapped, "a Brandy Alexander. I could hop out to the Blarney Stone we passed—off 39th—and bring it back."

Instinctively, Jack firmly replied, "No."

"Why," she taunted childlike, "you afraid I'm gonna cut out with the cash? I'll leave my nice, warm coat here."

It might be warm, thought Jack, but its nice days were gone. "No," he repeated. He knew, she'd observed his cash wad when he paid. That he was left only with twenties. Get a twenty off him, she probably figured, grab her coat, and when he tries to stop her, start screaming how on this cold winter's night this bastard's taking her coat. A situation, from which, he'd walk away.

Shaking her head, sympathetically, side to side, she now advised, "You have to learn to trust!"

He was still laughing when, back, back behind the eyes, jolted back, was he, to the Bronx—

The alley, back of the strip of six-story apartment buildings on Cruger Avenue, the block he grew up on located less than a short block from the number 2 train Pelham Parkway stop on the el, was narrow but long as a football field. Blocked in on all sides by six-story buildings, it was a long slab of sunless concrete. A long, tall fence backed-up by barking dogs fortified the buildings on the other side of the alley. "The Beast," or "Dirty Deuce," as the graffiti covered number 2 train was known, screeched thunderously by every five or so minutes. Its sheer force rocking the skeletal systems of all creatures of vertebrae within that one short block radius. Which included THE ALLEY—

Where son of a cop Clay Phelan hanged cats from fire escapes.

Where soft-spoken Spanish Bill, old and slightly stooped but tall still, in his weathered black ten-gallon cowboy hat, would fix bikes for boys free of charge in hopes of rounding-up a boy from whom he could gain sexual favors.

Where the basement dwelling inbred Woolfolk clan would picnic, between dripping first floor clotheslines beneath a downpour of chimney soot.

Where the ghostly white haired cat-lady would lay food for strays, mumbling about being fired from her job as a Radio City Music Hall Rockette because she refused to spread her legs for Frank Sinatra.

Where Jack joined the chorus of hyenas howling, "PINK BELLY!! PINK BELLY...!!" As they ripped the shirt from a crying boy's back, held him down and took turns SMACK! SMACK! SMACK!! Palm prints, blood streaked, raw, red belly. Laughing Jack, thankful it wasn't him on the receiving end.

Where a guy could take a piss.

Where that angel dust loving, rotten toothed, mudslide, Gerald Fiorino casually approached Jack as he practiced flipping baseball cards and called him a Jew bastard before cold-cocking him with a hip driven left hook to the ear. Five days, counted Jack, till the ear stopped ringing. Kept it to himself. Blessed revenge, he never got.

And where that same motherfucker Gerald Fiorino, arm slung around the slim shoulders of Natalie Ragovey, descended, with her, into. But, not before spotting Jack and Szyk hanging out about ten parked cars down the same side of the block. So he stopped along the way to jerk her tightly to him, whisper in her ear, and showcase a long kiss. Head fixed straight, Jack pretended not to see them. Observing the couple only from the corner of his thirteen year old eye. He would not give hated and feared Fiorino the in-your-face satisfaction.

Jack considered Natalie, who was a year ahead of him in eighth grade and lived directly across the street from him, to be a nice girl and cute. Curvy, with wild brown curls and gumball eyes. When crossing paths, she and Jack would often smile hello. And now she goes down into the alley with Gerald Fiorino! Nice, thought Jack, to press a girl like Natalie up against you. Tongue her. Really, though...how could she be with that piece of fucking shit?! Why not just jerk-off a dog, Jill Conklin did.

Mouth agape, squeezing a Spaldeen that he'd previously been bouncing, Jack turned to his equally freaked-out friend Szyk, who stood next to him leaning his backside on a parked car and stabbing Jack's stickball bat into the pavement, and exclaimed, "Oh fuck, Szyk, she's now the 'Kiss of Death'!"

And Fiorino was a dirtbag even by dirtbag standards and word got out.

To Jack's amazement, Natalie became known to all as the Kiss of Death. And proceeded to live up to her new name, fucking, sucking, and drugging, with assorted scumbags before being sent away somewhere by her family. Never again to be seen in the neighborhood, since a few weeks later the family Ragovey (her grandmother) moved out.

It can't be her. Well it could, but for that matter it could be one of a million similar looking girls. Hell, it has been like twenty years. Besides, the wacko eyes on this crazed bitch are like nothing I've ever seen.

Looking at him as she chewed her chicken and pork fried rice, he looked into her free floating big brown eyes a moment and it hit him. These gumballs were Natalie Ragovey's, short-circuited!

"I can give you a nice cheap blow job when we're done," she offered.

"No," replied Jack. Wondering why he should even care if it is her.

She persisted, "I'm disease free."

"I'm not afraid of disease," replied Jack dismissively, "though for a while I was afraid of going bald." In a casual manner, he then asked, "What's your name?"

"Gemini," she answered.

"Really!" Jack Barish suddenly demanded.

"All right, Natalia. What the fuck do you care anyway?"

Close enough, thought Jack, before replying condescendingly, "Actually, I don't. I'm just making conversation." For a fleeting moment, he did, however, feel genuinely bad for her. But not as bad as he now felt about this entire random meeting. There was no upside to her. All she did was bring him down. Didn't even pretend to listen to the revelations of Rocky. *Is it my fault this crazy bitch decided to make it with Gerald Fiorino?* She was a piece of shit loser, concluded Jack, irredeemably fucked-up well before he ever saw Rocky. Working himself into a muted rage against the entire pre-Rocky period of his life, which he wished to forget, and *this Natalie creature*, came easily.

Rising to her feet, she said, "I'm gonna use the bathroom. That is, if they let me. You know, there ought to be a law against these chink take-out joints that have tables but don't provide paying customers with toilet facilities."

Sitting there, he considered cutting out. Leave now, he thought, before she reappears. But, an opportunist could very well slip in and snatch her unattended coat from the back of the chair. A minute had quietly passed, so they must have allowed her in back. Despite the vague hatred for her that stirred within him, he didn't wish for *the skank* to end up coatless in the cold winter's night. A couple minutes more, he sat—

"And what's your name?" she asked dreamily hovering over him on her way back to her seat.

"Ger—ald," Jack offered up, darkly self-amused.

Shouting, "HE RAPED ME!!" down she pounced, onto his face, "YOU LOUSY PUNK BASTARD!!" biting and clawing, "YOU—NAMED ME!!" her hands clamped tight onto his ears, "HE RAPED ME!! YOU COULD'VE SAVED ME!!" And before he could overpower her, into his mouth, her tongue, she jammed, deep down—

COMMON GROUND

Like Godzilla vs. King Kong, the clash between Joe Proletariat and his landlord was inevitable. Proletariat (a tightly wound, slightly hunched, medium-sized, fifty-two-year-old bachelor), was a card carrying communist with exceptionally long arms. Aside from his very long arms, which may have been the result of decades of carrying shopping bags filled with used books, he was an ordinary- looking, gray-complexioned, white man.

A lifelong Brooklynite, Proletariat was now living in an apartment at 1606 Purdy Street, in the Parkchester section of the Bronx for one year. He made the move in order to be close to his job reassignment, within the Bureau of Motor Vehicles, at its East Tremont location. The reassignment involved a decent pay raise; and besides, after sixteen years in the same apartment he felt it was time for a change. So Proletariat and a comrade loaded a fairly large rented truck to absolute capacity with his belongings and moved him from his multi-racial Brooklyn neighborhood to one in the Bronx. Proletariat, a tightwad, could've easily afforded to hire movers, but you don't amass over $291,000 in savings from a lifetime in civil service by doing that. Every penny spent was filtered through a hyper-vigilant cash consciousness.

For his political causes, he did good work. Like collecting discarded eye-glass frames from retail optical establishments, for shipment to Cuba. High-end frames, however, he held on to. He went to Nicaragua, and aided the Sandinistas. In Manhattan's Central Park, for himself, he rolled up his sleeves to snatch coins from the bottom of the shallow water of the Bethesda Fountain. Coins tossed for good luck by whimsical pedestrians.

The day Proletariat moved from his Brooklyn apartment, his old landlord was moved to make love to his wife for the first time in fifteen years. Proletariat had made it a point to know all his rights as a tenant. *Landlord.* Even as a kid, he was repulsed by that word. What made some asshole lord of the land? What the fuck was this anyway? Feudalism?

The first seven months at his Bronx apartment all was OK. Heat and hot water. He got to know neighbors. Roaches and occasional mice were of no concern to him. For the first time since the almost decade old collapse of the Soviet Union, a day or two would now sometimes pass without him feeling depressed by it.

He became friendly with a fellow fifty-plus bachelor neighbor. A tall, gaunt, unemployed, Australian expatriate, Kevin Skelly, who, although apolitical, shared his passion for the strictly solo activities of sniffing through every inch of thrift shops and opportunistic street scavenging. Proletariat, for the most part, was able to limit his acquisitions to items he might actually use someday, and those which he deemed valuable. The Aussie was out of control. From old televisions to a prosthetic leg, from floor to ceiling piles of dust smothered books to stacks of wooden orange crates packed with record albums, to his gang of cats, his large apartment was navigable only by moving crabwise and cautiously. When it came to unavoidable retail purchases, they were attitudinal twins. Quantity over quality: single-ply toilet paper, canned corn beef, and plenty of sugar packets with coffee to go.

Proletariat always got a kick out of the Aussie's insane clutter. Seeing it helped him keep his own propensity for it under control, by serving as a reminder of the ultimate clutter horror. He limited his own thrift shop buys and street salvage to things he could rationalize, like a seven rotary phone backup. Anyhow, he genuinely liked the mild-mannered Aussie, and when the landlord moved to evict Skelly, at the behest of three tenants complaining about the stench created by his sixteen cats, Proletariat became incensed. "You *don't* put a guy out on the fucking street!" Loath to take one of his plentiful accumulated days off, he made a pledge to his drooping friend to intervene in the problem if things did not go his way.

The housing court judge ruled to give the Aussie two weeks to get rid of most of the cats, and rectify his odorous living situation. A hearing date was then scheduled for three weeks. In the interim between weeks two and three, a health inspector would make a home visit to the Aussie. Although this seemed fair enough to Proletariat, his hatred for landlords had been triggered. In an even more heightened state of landlord abuse mindfulness than usual, he noticed that the hot water was very hot. Immediately after being turned on. Too damn hot. He would check into it.

At Proletariat's urging, the Aussie got rid of ten of his cats. After making dozens of calls he succeeded in finding new homes for only three. The remaining seven, he took out to Queens, to the shelter at the Center for Animal Care and Control. The volunteer there was a hefty white woman with a mane of wild gray hair and Sixties style, small and circular granny-glasses. She had no sympathy for the heartfelt pain he expressed at being forced to part with the majority of his beloved cats. The cats she regarded lovingly, with a sense of awe. As though each meowing box was a self-consuming burning bush. But, reacted to his profound sadness with disdain. And even though he had handed her a one hundred dollar check, in full payment of her agency fee, she refused to give him a receipt. He wanted the receipt to show the health inspector who would be visiting his apartment. But the events of the day had left him so dejected he meekly departed, perplexed. Clueless, that the divine love this woman displayed for cats was only cover for an even greater passion—hatred of men!

Further urging by Proletariat sparked the Aussie to work diligently in an attempt to clean the entire apartment, working around the awesome clutter as best he could. Skelly became vigilant about keeping the kitty litter-boxes as fresh as possible. Previously, he had indeed been negligent. The future was anyone's guess. Presently, he kept cloying cherry incense burning all day.

Friday of the second week, three days after the health inspector's visit, the Aussie received notice that the apartment *passed* inspection. His relief, however, would be short-lived, because in Monday's mail he received a letter from the court stating that the hearing date, which was for tomorrow, remained in effect. The landlord, now with the aid of a lone tenant and a lawyer on retainer, had persisted in following through with the hearing.

Early that evening the Aussie, appearing strangely calm, almost resigned, informed Proletariat. Figuring that the positive inspection had rendered the hearing moot, Proletariat was shocked and outraged that the landlord was pressing on (even though he knew that the landlord had nothing to lose and plenty to gain). If the landlord could vacate that apartment he could substantially increase the rent. Proletariat assured his friend that he, Joe Proletariat, would join him tomorrow on his behalf as a witness at the hearing. This was war.

That night Proletariat recruited for the cause another loner tenant, Ray Ortiz, with whom he was friendly. The low-key, unionized hospital worker barely knew the Aussie. But after a full hour Proletariat briefing, Ortiz agreed to join with them and appear as a pro-Aussie character witness at tomorrow's Housing Court hearing.

Leaving Ortiz' apartment on the second floor, Proletariat got on the elevator and found himself alone with the sole remaining tenant complainant. An attractive, well-dressed, twenty-something, Hispanic single-mother who lived in a third-floor studio apartment with her little boy. As he entered, she acknowledged him with a polite smile of recognition. "You!" Proletariat declared instantly, "are a disreputable agent of the landlord, who will someday be judged by the highest authority of all, God!" An atheist, Proletariat always enjoyed bringing God into it when arguing morality with anyone he deemed to be a believer.

"Blow me!" she shouted into his face as the elevator stopped at three, perfectly timed, by chance, for her departure.

"Blow me?" he mumbled to himself. "Blow me?" he repeated incredulously. Shutting up into his head with, "Why that little fucking cunt!" Feeling somehow violated, he stomped off, at his floor.

And late that night, still agitated by her words, Proletariat, who usually slept very well, could not fall asleep. Sitting up in bed, he considered getting up to read at his living room desk. He got up and, as was his custom, he nodded over at the life-size wooden Indian that faced him from a far corner of his room—indigenous, loyal, and without maintenance cost.

Once in the living room, Proletariat's mental gears shifted from reading to an even higher mode of comfort—the fellatio-of-self mode of assessing the probable value of recently thrifted or scavenged acquisitions.

On top of the modest armoire that he salvaged while walking through Brooklyn Heights back in 1984, rested two recent acquisitions. One, which was what he correctly believed to be the first English edition (London, 1886) of Dostoyevsky's *Crime and Punishment*. A must sell, since he could not in good conscience keep in his home a book by an author whose politics he considered reactionary. The other, a cut-glass decanter that he bought at a nearby thrift shop for five dollars, because he guessed it was very old and worth ten times that. But guess was all he could do, since, unlike books, which he certainly knew, he knew next to nothing about glass. He took it into the kitchen to admire under the bright kitchen light and was moved to rinse it. Held it under the faucet, turned right to hot, it cracked. Three imperfect lines coming together at a point, like a chicken's foot, only longer. Extremely agitated, Proletariat suffered through a sleepless night. Brain locked on receiving financial compensation for this valuable decanter from the landlord due to the excessively hot water.

At seven-thirty the next morning, sleepless but filled with purpose, Proletariat ran down the building superintendent and insisted he inspect the damage to the decanter. The super accompanied him up to his apartment and witnessed the cracked decanter. Proletariat then had himself a cup of instant coffee, extra heavy on the glommed sugar, before indiscriminately throwing on one of several second-generation sport jackets, and heading out on this drab early March morning, to meet the Aussie and Ortiz. For now, the matter of the damaged decanter had to be put aside. *But, right after the hearing...!*

The grateful Aussie announced that he'd pick up the tab for a cab. Proletariat immediately hailed a gypsy cab. And the three men were transported to the old and very large State Supreme Court building on the Grand Concourse, which overlooked Yankee Stadium.

The assigned hearing chamber was a relatively small, stark room, presided by a fully-robed, elderly black male judge. The sole remaining tenant complainant, the young Hispanic woman who had out scored Proletariat in last night's elevator tell-off, was a no-show. Only the attorney appeared for the landlord. Enormous, baby-faced, and perfectly circular, the attorney's physical appearance amazed Proletariat. Six feet circumference in three-piece pinstripe containment. Proletariat sensed that the judge was perturbed at the attorney for his insistence on pursuing the matter despite the non-appearance of any tenant complainants. A pleasurable realization dawned suddenly on Proletariat—This big circle that was attorney couldn't possibly obtain such oversized clothing for a penny less than retail!

The Aussie, who retained no legal counsel, stammered some, but handled himself pretty well on the stand. He simply was truthful. Ortiz was never called. Feeling very oppressed and pissed off, Proletariat was. The following exchanges between him and the landlord's attorney highlighted his brief appearance on the stand:

"Mr. Proletariat," stated the boyish voiced attorney, "you claim to visit Mr. Skelly regularly in his apartment. I ask you. Is there any trace of foul odor?"

Proletariat responded by fussily removing an asthma inhaler from an inner pocket of his jacket, and using it. Showcasing his particular vulnerability to any cat abundance. In actuality, he had not been bothered by asthma for years. "No," was all he said.

Unfazed, the attorney posed another question: "Is it not possible, Mr. Proletariat, for Mr. Skelly to deposit his cats into closets prior to your arrival?"

"No," replied Proletariat.

"No? Why not?" asked the attorney.

"Kevin Skelly has no phone. All my visits are unannounced," Proletariat replied, feigning aloofness.

"Yet!" snapped the attorney in a tone of triumph, as though Proletariat's last response was what he had anticipated, "these cats may be closeted and would that not, in fact, curtail any odor?"

Proletariat paused. "I don't know," he condescended, "I'm not an expert on permeation of odor through doors." No longer willing or able to veil his contempt, on he spoke, "If you wanna know, why don't you station yourself right outside the closed door to the men's room for awhile and sniff around?"

The judge ruled in favor of the Aussie, who profusely thanked Proletariat and Ortiz. Handshakes completed, each of the three men headed off in separate directions. Proletariat took the subway straight home.

Walking through his front door, he tossed his jacket aside, grabbed the large Yellow Pages directory from a closet, his personal address book from his desk, and started dialing his trusty black rotary phone and sat down to complete the call.

First he called the landlord's office. It was not much past noon, yet there was no pick-up. So he left a short but firm message requesting the landlord, a Hassidic Jew by the name of M.(what the M. stood for nobody knew) Bluefarb, to return his call ASAP.

An hour's worth of phone directory thumbing and calls, revealed that the Department of Housing Preservation and Development was the government agency within whose jurisdiction the too-hot water problem fell. Relentlessly, Proletariat re-dialed that number throughout a half hour of busy signals, finally penetrating the recordings to a live voice. Keeping his balance as he was shuffled around from one person to the next, his tone highly civil, requesting always to be transferred not hung up on, his bureaucratic game plan was intact: To stay on the line until he got someone on the other end whom he could somehow stick to and wear down. And although there was no record of any other 1606 Purdy Ave. tenant complaints to the agency in this regard, he was able to prevail upon a soft-spoken bureaucrat, convincing him of the urgency of the situation. "First thing tomorrow," he assured Proletariat, "an inspector will be by." Proletariat then piled two more calls onto the landlord's answering machine, knowing full well that the first message had very likely been received and one or one thousand messages he would not get a call back today.

Next morning just before eight o'clock, while waiting for the inspector, he again called the landlord's office. Much to Proletariat's surprise, "Bluefarb speaking," is what he got on the first ring.

"Bluefarb, this is 1606 Purdy, 5P—Proletariat."

"So," interjected Bluefarb, very calmly, "Mr. Proletariat, what can I do for you?"

"Mr. Bluefarb," stated Proletariat, "I am sure by now you are aware of the damage to my cut-glass decanter, a valuable heirloom of incalculable sentimental worth, which resulted from the hazardous hot water condition here at 1606 Purdy Ave. As a result, I intend on taking a two hundred dollar rent deduction next month. I also intend to notify the proper authorities." Proletariat was pleased with the matter-of-fact tone and content of his delivery. He had, of course, already notified the authorities, and awaited the inspector's arrival even as he spoke.

"You are the only one with such a complaint," replied Bluefarb, sounding puzzled by such an unlikelihood.

"That sir, is beside the point," replied Proletariat, slightly annoyed.

"Why don't you simply turn the cold on first, and adjust?" asked Bluefarb.

"I've been doing it this way my entire life!" Proletariat replied defensively.

"Is it my fault that you can't change a habit?" And with that M. Bluefarb gently hung up on Joe Proletariat.

The Talmudic scholar had landed a forceful blow against the dialectical materialist, and some thirty seconds later Proletariat was still stunned, when the loud ding-dong of his doorbell snapped him out of it. It was the inspector from the Department of Housing Preservation and Development. Using a special thermometer, the inspector recorded the hot water temperature at one hundred ninety degrees Fahrenheit. *Sixty degrees higher than the maximum allowed!* It was a buoyant Proletariat that left for work that morning.

As soon as he sat down at his desk, he pushed all job related business aside and hurriedly wrote a letter to Bluefarb. After a very early lunch break, walked over to the Post Office and bought a stamp. Having affixed the stamp to the sealed envelope, he self-satisfiedly dropped it into the appropriate mail slot. Ordinarily, he'd have waited till the end of the work day (as he always did with all his personal mail), in order to slip it, undetected, through the office postage meter. However, this particular matter so pressed on him that he could not hold off taking care of it for even a minute longer. The letter read as follows:

March 14, 2002

Dear Mr. Bluefarb:

A senior inspector from the Department of Housing Preservation and Development was here, in my apartment. He substantiated my claim about the hazardous hot water. You will be hearing from them. There are also many other housing and health code violations here at 1606 Purdy Avenue, such as a roach infestation in the basement and near the openings to the incinerators. I will be reporting this to the proper New York City agencies after giving you proper due warning. When I moved to 1606 Purdy Avenue I expected and wanted to live a quiet and tranquil life. However, due to your insolence and greed this has not been possible. With his own eyes your building superintendent witnessed the destruction from scalding (near the boiling point) water of a priceless decanter which belonged to my great-grandmother. After several unanswered calls to your office I had to report this dangerous problem to the proper city agency. You'll have to have this fixed! This is a serious problem which could result in the scalding of human flesh belonging especially to children and senior citizens. I hereby request you call me at home any morning within ten days of the date of this letter, before eight-thirty at (718) 654-4566 to discuss compensation for my destroyed heirloom. In the interest of expediency I will accept two hundred dollars to put this loss behind me. I will not allow you to harass me or my fellow tenants, like when you heinously attempted to evict my friend Kevin Skelly on spurious grounds and lost out in court. Someday, as all of us will, you too will be judged by the highest authority of all: God Himself!

Sincerely Yours,
Joe Proletariat

cc: files

Two days later, as he walked out of his front door for work that morning, Proletariat's phone rang. In he rushed and on the lull following ring two grabbed it, "HEL—LO!" "Is that you, Proletariat?" asked Bluefarb.

"Yes."

"This is Mr. Bluefarb. Listen, I'm willing to do something for you Mr. Proletariat, but I cannot accept any responsibility on your loss. And you've got to behave yourself."

"*Behave myself?*" Proletariat echoed incredulously, realizing full well that was not possible.

"You can deduct twenty-five dollars from next month's rent, and an additional twenty-five the following month, for a total of fifty dollars," said Bluefarb.

Remarkably, this amount coincided perfectly with the ten times the purchase price formula Proletariat contrived to assess the decanter when he purchased it. And before Proletariat could utter a word, Bluefarb emphatically added, "Look, we both *know* that eighty-five percent of life is money."

"It's a deal," replied Proletariat, finding himself intuitively in total agreement with this precise money/life calculation. A calculation he himself had never consciously explored.

How would each man break down the remaining fifteen percent? Nobody knows.

GODFATHER DEATH

Based on the brothers Grimm fairy tale.

All the days and all the nights, a poor man slaved to feed all his little ones. But when the thirteenth was born, he cried. Not enough hours in the day to earn for another one. So he took off down the road to find a godfather for the boy. A road one goes alone.

Like a foot soldier, he marched. On and on...night was empty as death. Then streaks of silver crossed the dark sky and the sickle moon turned shocking blue—and a beat up old Honda Civic cutoff his path. No driver! Through a crack in the muffler thundered an otherworldly command: "I AM GOD AND I WILL WATCH OVER YOUR SON AND HE WILL THRIVE!"

"If I were you," replied the poor man flatly, "I too, would be ashamed to show my face." And the poor man marched on, wondering why God chose to project from inside the muffler. Why not through the exhaust pipe? It would seem to make more sense. Many miles later he stopped, and urinated into some bushes...

Speckled with droplets, a five-and-a-half-foot-long, fat, scaly, red serpent with a man-shaped head slithered forth from beneath the freshly drenched bush. The serpent rose. Its head was that of a man, its face that of a very ordinary middle-aged man.

"I'm sorry!" exclaimed the poor man.

"Don't sweat it. I lay in wait for you but fell asleep. Lucky for your son, the golden shower woke me. For I am the devil, and I will watch over your son and he will thrive. He will fuck anything that moves and die with the most toys."

"Fucking anything that moves," replied the poor man. "Well, I don't know about that, but I certainly don't believe whoever dies with the most toys wins."

And he marched on and on . . .

Towards a loner who marched towards him. Bones on bones. A skeleton. Clickety-clack-click. Death had come to pitch. "I am Death and I will watch o—"

"Yes!" interrupted the poor man. "Yes! Everybody dies. Homer died. Dante died. Madonna will die."

Godfather Death watched over the boy. He became a great doctor. One who could cure the gravely ill. For Godfather Death had provided him with an occult potion. A universal cure. Along with conditions. If the rattling skeletal hand of his godfather appeared above the head of the bedridden—the potion should be given. If it appeared at the foot of the bed—Classic Coke should be given. Godfather Death graciously allowed a fifty-fifty live or die split. And advised his godson never to disobey the conditions, because the punishment would be his life.

The great doctor lacked for nothing. Cash and classy ladies in abundance. Yet he always made time to aid the poor. So when a musty old woman hunched over an empty shopping cart knocked on his door, and begged him to make a house call to her dying 17-year-old granddaughter, he hailed a cab and off they went.

The ridged contours of the drab woolen blanket that the doctor looked down upon hid the frail girl under it. Only honey-colored hair and a small chalky forehead were uncovered. From beneath the blanket came her muffled song—a lullaby. And it thrilled him. Thrilled him to tears. She, he resolved instantly, would be his wife. But the rattling skeletal hand appeared at the foot of her bed. Quickly he tore off the blanket, and spun her like a bottle. The skeletal hand now appeared above her head. And he gave her the potion . . .

Godfather Death summoned him. Ordered his godson the doctor to meet him way down an abandoned coal mine in Boone County, West Virginia. There stood Godfather Death. Amid a deep circle of flickering candles. Perfect posture. Arms crossed. A big-boned son of a gun.

"It won't happen again," said his godson.

"Especially not if you're dead," replied Godfather Death. He then posed a question to him. "Godson, if you had to choose between remaining the great doctor I made you or making this girl your wife—which would you choose?"

"The girl," replied the godson.

"That is the better choice," said Godfather Death. "But if I were you, I wouldn't make any plans beyond exactly two years and one minute from right now..."

Scapegoat

The team of fifteen-year-old softballers taking the field of cement that July afternoon, for an unorganized schoolyard contest at P.S.105 in the Bronx, was not a good one. Our first baseman, Rob Warren, was a jump-shooting basketball phenom. Irving from Texas, our shortstop, was a quick-fisted, manly, cross between Joe Namath and Elvis, and a consummate "getter" of girls. But good softball players, not one. No spastics, just unskilled and undisciplined.

I was in my head at second base, brain locked on "Hello Goodbye" by the Beatles: "'hello, hello / I don't know why you say goodbye / I say hello / hello, hello / I don't know why you say goodbye / I say hello ...'"

I don't think we had a right fielder, and the "official pitcher" (one who pitches to both sides) was a hulking seventeen-year-old, red-headed tomboy—Gilda. She also served as the lone umpire. A good ballplayer, she was looking for a guy to play stickball against when we drafted her. She agreed because she got to hone her pitching skills, and be at the center of the action.

At third base was barrel-chested pinhead "Little Rosie," Jeff Rosenblatt. He had an older pot dealing brother, Fred, who at 5'6" and close to three-hundred pounds was "Big Rosie."

Big Rosie dealt quantity. He was partners in pot dealing with their father. They kept fifteen-hundred dollars operating cash stashed underneath a floorboard in the foyer of their apartment.

Last summer, as fire raged through their building, Big Rosie and the father stood outside the evacuated building FREAKING about the cash. The firefighters held their own battling the fire. Two minutes later Little Rosie showed up, to eat. His father and big brother quickly convinced him to mad dash into the burning building to fetch the cash. He did, and he rescued the cash. Some boys laughed in his face over that. Others, behind his back.

Catching was a profanity-spewing fire hydrant named Eugene, who by inserting two fingers into his mouth could produce an ear-quaking whistle. He could also "clam" at will. That is, sounding like an air gun, he'd expectorate a glob of clammy missile. In center was some kid Irv grabbed off the street. And in left, was a favorite target of every bully—Neil Fogelfish. A fair sized boy who got "beat on" regularly because he did not retaliate. He was—"Feesh."

The opposing team was a bunch from across the Bruckner Expressway. I didn't know any of them. They appeared to be around our age but did not go to the same school as us. A couple of our guys seemed to know a couple of their guys. Which is probably how the game came together. What I did know, after two innings, was that they were no better than us.

In the top of the third we're ahead 4-3, but with one out, they load the bases. The batter hits a high hopper to short that our third baseman Little Rosie manages to cut-off and flip to me at second for one and I fire to first where Rob Warren stretches like a major leaguer to scoop up my low hard throw. This miraculously executed double play splendor would have ended the inning, but Gilda called the close play at first in favor of the runner. Her call was correct. As Rob was getting to his feet one run had already scored, knotting it at 4, and their three base runners were buffalo STAMPEDING around the base paths. In an attempt to head off the go ahead run, he unleashed a furious throw in the general direction of home plate that hit the runner heading home in the head with a THUD collapsing him like a sack of bricks and triggering our team collective unconscious.

Led by the left side of our infield, we rushed out to left field—to beat on Feesh—who earlier in the game had committed an inconsequential error. GAME OVER.

On Maxie Off

The Background

Some people have no sense of time. Such a person was Maxie Pomerantz. He was ALWAYS late. That's if he showed up at all. As a result of this personality trait, at around thirteen years of age he became known in our Bronx neighborhood as "Maxie Off." Or simply—"Off." Years later, a local drug-dealer theorized that a piece of Maxie's brain had to be missing. But I knew better. His brain was cool. He just didn't give a fuck about what time it was. Never did. Whatever he was doing: smoking weed, scheming, handicapping the ponies, or sleeping—he'd be totally into it. Nothing else mattered. His existence transcended the ordinariness of time. He had innate intelligence and a good heart. But an inability to do an HONEST days work. It was impossible for him. More on that later. The first time I met him—

I was seated toward the front of the classroom in seventh-grade, on the first day of the 1971 school year, as the teacher, Mr. Howser, sternly addressed us hushed students. He was feeling us out, and we were feeling him out. From the back of the class I hear—

HA!
HA!!
HA!

Three loud unrestrained mono-syllabic blasts of laughter—the second the loudest.

I turn around. It was this kid Maxie Pomerantz, laughing openly—in the teacher's face. Over who knows what?

He was told to shut up, and two laugh blasts later, he did.

After I got to know Maxie, I came to realize that he wasn't trying to show the teacher up. He just laughed, heartily, whenever—the fuck—he found something funny, and didn't CARE to know better.

Long as I knew him, the ten years to follow, this did not change. Nor did any of the aforementioned features of his personality ever change. This combination of qualities propelled him to legendary exploits. As these exploits mounted, his name further evolved and split off into the more formal—"the Officer." "The Officer" could be used interchangeably with "Off" or "Maxie Off." Depending on one's arbitrary impulse, at any moment in time.

The Root of Pathology

Six-two and about 200 lbs. at twenty-two, the Officer was an imposing guy. He had green eyes and thick, wavy black hair. But, his head was too small for his body, his complexion sallow, and his hips too wide for his shoulders. Nevertheless, he could dunk a basketball.

Since his conviction the year before (on a felony to which he pleaded guilty and got five years probation), he seemed much older. Although, I could not put my finger on what it was about him that changed. Maybe I changed.

He loved a buck. That could NEVER change. He HAD TO have it. Had to have it for gambling, drugs, gas, and girls. But, he did not like work. When it came to making a buck he HAD TO detour at the law, or break it.

So, he and I are sitting on the dirty green carpeted floor in his room, upstairs in his parents' very modest Bronx home. A home he had yet to move from. Sitting around smoking pot and Marlboros, watching the Knicks play the 76ers on channel 9, in 1981. We needed Knicks. I was down for fifty bucks. Phoned it into a bookie.

Maxie Off's credit was no good, anywhere. But, since he made big punches—five hundred bucks a pop—one bookie, hungry for Off's action, would dispatch one of his long-ago broken losers, as a footman, to meet Off and get cash—up front.

I was already high on Seconal. We took hits of his mediocre coke intermittently. The game was tight and the dark smoky room our clearly defined world. We needed Knicks. No knock—the door swings open. A bare flabby arm of a woman—BANANA—held in hand—is all that enters—a bare flabby arm of a woman—BANANA—held in hand—"Maxie, nem* a banana!" The voice—his Polish Jewish mother, presenting her Maxala—A PERFECT YELLOW BANANA!

The Deeds

The window in the men's room at the Howard Johnson—across from the Bronx Zoo on Southern Boulevard—could be slid up no more than a foot. So, in order for Off to get each five-gallon cardboard cylinder—containing ice cream—out through the window, he had to position them horizontally, before dropping them into the back alley. Where he'd go collect them after punching out on Sundays when his shift—bussing tables—was done for the day. Off would then carry the ice-cold containers down the block and around the corner to a local luncheon-

---

* Yiddish - *take*

ette, where they were very happy to get Howard Johnson ice-cream, real cheap.

The job at Howard Johnson also required him to fill-in as cashier. Off mastered the cash register, and the opportunities it afforded him—to steal, real quick. The cash register became his "piano" and he, a virtuoso. It was a talent which served him well, in all future employment, where he was called upon to cashier.

That was Maxie Off's first job—after turning sixteen—and getting his working papers. He had no vices to support—yet. Nor, did he lack for anything at home. Off figured, "Everybody steals." And, "Fuck those Jew-haters, anyway." Two elements which, in combination with one another, produce one powerfully compounded solid position.

XXXXXXXXXX

Off had only a learner's permit to drive when the tall seventeen-year-old somehow managed to get hired as deliveryman for Blue-Star Kosher Butchers. He was to drive their van, delivering orders of meat to customers, and collecting payment for these meats. He did. He also smuggled meat out of the store and sold it. And regularly fleeced Blue-Star of cash, sharply maneuvering, as handler of their cash. He figured, "Fuck those cheap Jews."

At night he'd steal the van and shoot up to Yonkers Raceway. He was hooked on horses. Smoked a loose one and shot his nuts playing ponies.

As with every job he ever had, after a few months, he was fired. Even when Maxie Off had a real good thing, his lateness was certain. As certain as the sunrise.

At eighteen, he got his driver's license. Within months, he was blacklisted by every yellow cab company in Manhattan. He'd show up late, work a few hours, take the cab to the track, get "robbed" and return the cab—empty-handed. Sometimes, right before returning the cab, he'd report the "robbery" to the local police precinct where he "got robbed."

A year later, Off bought a used two-door, red, black-top, fastback Cutlass. A sharp car, never to be washed again. We could now shoot to Roosevelt Raceway out on Long Island. Crossing the Whitestone Bridge, we'd look for an unblocked, out-of-operation automated tollbooth, whose wooden arm—that was supposed to be down—was in the up position. Conditioned drivers would stop their cars by the metal basket and mindlessly drop their coins into it. We'd go right through— never paying. Maxie Off spotted this—instantly—for the set-up that it was. Unaccounted monies collected, to be split-up among "the boys" working that shift.

Sometimes, coming back, if no toll was set-up for the boys, the Officer would drive right through a manned booth, slapping his empty hand hard against the toll collector's open palm—

HA!

HA!!

HA!

Done—and never caught. After we won at the track or lost.

xxxxxxxxxx

Never a lucky gambler, he was a good handicapper. And, for a week or two, could get very hot. During these scientifically (as opposed to luck) fueled hot streaks, I only had to reach into my pocket to cover my own bets. Diner costs, track admissions and programs, bar tabs and pot, he covered. But money in his pocket did not mean payment for his creditors. Unless, he was confronted with imminent physical danger by capable bone-breakers, he wasn't paying anyone.

One winning night, we're up in the clubhouse at Yonkers Raceway, and on this Saturday night even the clubhouse is packed. We're standing underneath one of the televised tote boards, smoking, handicapping, and occasionally looking up at the televised tote board, when a cologne-soaked, rhino-necked enforcer spots the Officer for someone, who he believes, has reneged on a couple hundred owed the storefront bookie joint, where the enforcer was one of several clerks. He believed right.

He comes over to where we're standing, "I know you!" he accusingly says to the Officer, as though the Officer was disguised as a tea-kettle, but couldn't fool him—his left index finger in Off's chest—

"WHAT'RE—YOU—SOME KIND OF HOMO?!" The Officer shouts into his face—and the eyes of the crowd of gamblers—some with girlfriends—fix upon a—now—confused and self-conscious enforcer—who slinks away shaking his head left to right to left . . .

The unshakable Officer sensed some uncertainty, and so, the cologne-soaked, rhino-necked enforcer was victimized by the master of reversion. He was not the first such victim, nor would he be the last.

xxxxxxxxxx

I unloaded the last of the truckload of large cartons, that had previously been packed by Off with one hundred small boxes of Kotex

107

sanitary napkins per carton, off of Off's rented truck. The owner of the South Bronx drug store, in front of which we were double-parked, was now doing a quick count of them as Off hovered over his back, bombing the bald top of the old druggist's radish-like head with bluish cigarette smoke exhalations. That each small sample box had imprinted on it SAMPLE—NOT FOR SALE mattered not, to the owner of drug stores. Grinning a self-congratulatory grin, he handed the Officer crisp cash, and we were gone.

This caper was made possible when a prominent marketing firm hired the Officer to manage a short-term project for them. He was to supervise the distribution of small sample boxes of Kotex sanitary napkins, throughout a slice of Westchester. They never bothered to check Off's fraudulent resumé. He, being naturally delusional, believed it. Why shouldn't they?

Not only were no samples distributed to the public, but also the entire amount allocated for payroll was paid to himself, under several aliases—and me. He was a generous guy. I got several paychecks for doing nothing, and I didn't even have to kickback. Over the next couple of days most all the money made from the Kotex sample box sale was "donated" to the track.

xxxxxxxxxx

No regulars at the track are winners. None. Losers all. The "game" grinds you into dust. With only loose change left between the two of us, after, another losing night, and the fuel indicator well below E, we were feeling very lucky just to make it back to the Bronx. Suddenly—a big black Buick Wildcat cuts us off—screeching smokily—to a stop—causing the Officer to slam the brakes on the Cutlass—bringing us to a similarly abrupt rubber-burning stop. The big black Wildcat is known to us—

A loose-built, long-haired giant emerges, in sections, from the driver's side. A regular-sized guy, wiry and blond, has jumped out the other side. The big guy is the Big Bluff, named in dishonor of his crappy poker game, and the other, cocksman turned junkie—Silverman. Tight-fisted, glowers pasted—the duo approaches. We've remained seated as they position themselves, one at each of our doors. The Big Bluff—the loose-built, long-haired giant by Off's door. And his smack-commando—Silverman—by mine.

"You got till Thursday to pay up!" Is the Bluff's ultimatum to the Officer, an ultimatum issued by the deep-toking marijuana marathoner through orthodontically adjusted horsy choppers—

HA!
HA!!
HA!

The Officer laughs right in his face.

Muttering—bloody Thursday threats—the Big Bluff and Silverman hop back into the Wildcat, and tear off under the El.

Apparently, Maxie Off buying the Big Bluff all the cereal he could eat, and then turning him on to super-potent sweet black opiated hash panacea, after the Bluff's parents threw their son out of the house last year, didn't count for much anymore to the towering former poker player, forever pot glutton—

HA!

HA!!

HA!

I couldn't stop laughing either.

XXXXXXXXXX

The Officer took a civil service test, scored on top, presented well at the interview, and was hired: by the New York State Dept. of Taxation and Finance—as a Tax-Compliance Agent. There couldn't have been much of a background check done. If there had been, several misdemeanor convictions would have been discovered. Just one month prior, he was arrested when police raided an abandoned Spanish Harlem building, where he was one of eighty-seven men arrested, betting on live dog-fights.

As a Tax-Compliance Agent, the twenty-year-old Maxie Off, was to visit businesses that were tax delinquent and effect collection. He had the power to seize bank accounts and shutdown businesses. On the days he was required to work in the office, he'd show-up late. As a result, he became the first and only agent ever to have to punch-in on the clock. This had no affect on his lateness.

However, when he was out in the field and actually worked, this bettor of horses, ballgames and dogs, would astound his supervisor with superior productivity. This, in spite of the fact that much of the time he was supposed to be out in the field working, he'd be home, asleep. He had added a new quinella to his repertoire: cocaine and girls.

Deeply seasoned in deceit, he was shy and green when it came to girls. He had yet to learn that girls did not have to be an expense. Gambling, drugs, and girls: a breakneck action box for the Officer.

Lots of cash was needed, for him to carry on. He began shaking-down tax debtors. Some, who knew they were being shook-down. Others, who knew they were being shook-down, but didn't want to know. And one who didn't even know he was being shook-down. In every case, cash to the Officer was cheaper than checks to the government. And the Officer mastered the art of the shakedown. However, his breakneck action box proved to be a natural disaster so ravenous, it overwhelmed even his artistry. He ended up copping a plea to a felony (the same felony mentioned earlier) and was sentenced to the five years probation and a $5,000 fine.

He spent the next several months amassing the cash, by dealing large amounts of Quaaludes he'd acquired from an acquaintance who was a pharmacist. The pharmacist was under pressure to support his wife and two children in a comfortable lifestyle. The Officer was under pressure to gamble, get high, and make payments on the fine. He did, however, get himself a couple low-maintenance girlfriends.

Epilogue

That was then. Today, the thirty-eight-year-old Officer lives in New Jersey with his wife Laura and their two children. They've been married for close to twelve years. The marriage has had some rocky spots, but they've always stayed together. He's toned down his gambling and only smokes pot.

Their two children, Larry (10 years old), and Cara (8), are adorable and appear to be doing well. Although, some say that the Officer puts undue pressure on skilled little Larry, drilling into the psyche of his young son Off's own living adolescent Yankee fantasy. His wife Laura runs her own small business, a local daycare center. Assisted by her staff of one, she handles everything. Her workday is long and exhausting.

The Officer works part-time, but earns more. He sells ad-space in community-watch newspapers that he publishes. This is his fifth year in this business. His is a one man operation. He is very adept at enabling potential customers to exhibit their civic responsibility, by kicking-in to support their community-watch paper. His unflappability, resolve and resourcefulness, combine to make his pitch a kind of customized voodoo. His success rate selling space to immigrant owners of retail establishments is exceptionally good. He regularly acquires new accounts, and although none of his customers have ever seen the ads they've paid for, many continue to advertise regularly. Actually, no one has ever seen any of the papers he publishes. Not even he.

Me, The Psychic Space Eater, and the Speech Therapist

He was a psychic space eater. From 50 feet, I could sense this about the bulky old man walking steadily down the block in the direction of the Second Avenue bus stop, where only I waited. Heavy presence. A type of person who simply cannot blend in, has to get noticed. Annoying, but basically harmless. On this cold, January day in Manhattan, his hands were buried in the pockets of his rumpled, putrescent-brown-colored, ankle-length raincoat. Some 20 feet from me, he came to a complete halt alongside a large, sitting, white mutt and its owner, a young woman in a long down coat and hood.

Broad faced, thick lipped, and bushy browed: Russian? His was the face of a genius or a fool. The odds did not favor the former. The stocking cap he wore was the same putrescent-brown as his raincoat. An impossible match. Maybe, he was a genius. He turned slightly left, looked down at the mutt, and beamed a grotesque, blissful smile at it. He seemed awestruck, smiling on, for 30 solid seconds, as though he were an ancient Hebrew witnessing the parting of the Red Sea. Still smiling that smile, he turned to face the mutt's owner. Blankly, she looked right through him. Brutal. Completely ignored him. Smiling no longer, he turned away.

He then approached the bus stop where I stood. A congregation of horseflies hovered just above of his head. As he drew closer, however, I could see that the horsefly congregation was actually extensive pilling from his stocking cap. At that moment the bus pulled up. And although I look through no one, I was very pleased not to have to deal with whatever he would inevitably have dealt. Especially, since a recent surgery left my right vocal cord paralyzed, rendering my voice an exhausting, breathy whisper. Naturally, he cut ahead of me and took an excessive amount of time to produce and swipe his MetroCard, and move on, blocking my entrance and keeping me out in the cold.

It was late morning and the bus mostly vacant. I walked to the middle, and before taking a seat, watched as he plopped into one of the seats up front by the driver. Only then did I take a left-side window seat. Four local stops and I get off. Nevertheless, I loosened my scarf and removed my Mets cap. First stop, 91st Street. Only one man boarded and took a seat in the rear. As the bus pulled out, the old psychic space eater rose to his feet and turned to the aisle. Staggering stiffly, sleep-walker-like, down the aisle of the moving bus, he came, this Frankenstein monster. Passing nothing but vacant seats, he plopped into the one right next to me. Like a jack-in-the-box, I popped up, and without so much as a glance moved to the back of the bus.

No energy for him. He remained seated.

At the 86th St. stop he again rose, and moved back to his original seat up front. I glanced out the window, focusing solely on storefront signs: Imperial Cleaners, Señor Swanky's, Serenity Nail Spa....Next stop, 79th Street, he got off. Because I was seated on the other side of the bus and chose to remain seated, I could not observe him from a window. At 72nd Street, I got off. And in less time than it takes to milk a cow, I was in the speech therapist's modest office for my second visit. On opposite sides of what looked to be a children's finger-painting table, she and I sat. Face to face.

Caroline Bell was an attractive, fortyish, mid-western blonde. Pale blue eyes and remarkably smooth skin. More importantly, she was competent and caring. She spoke unaffected American in a girlish voice. The quality of which was well represented by her last name. A voice of which I can't ever imagine tiring of. She asked me if I had practiced the exercises at home. Exercises like the one with which we would soon begin—while pressing my palms together and turning head left, rasping "E-e-e-e-e-e" 3 times, with breaths in between. I nodded affirmatively. A total lie. Once I found out the work I was doing with her was intended to make things more bearable for now, but had no restorative effect on the paralyzed vocal cord, I didn't even bother. She demonstrated a vocal exercise. I repeated it: Exercise after exercise. From across the small table, she kept her eyes on me. I began to feel special, like a little boy who is the sole object of his lovely kindergarten teacher's attention. She paused to ask me what I was doing for the scar on my neck. Mutely, I held my palms up and casually shrugged as if to say, Huh, what am I supposed to be doing? "Cocoa butter in slow circular motions," she replied. "Slow circular motions." She was concerned with the corrugated garter snake of a scar across my neck. I was not. So what if it looked as though my neck had been opened using a beer can opener? I was solely concerned with coming out on the right side of the 50/50 odds of my voice returning. That left no one to be concerned about the next phase of the cancer treatment.

I must've just missed the bus at 72nd Street, because there was no one waiting. Preferring not to remain standing in the cold, I lowered my head and, leaning slightly forward, put one foot in front of the other, weaving through the human traffic at a deliberate pace. Not nearly recovered from the neck surgery, by 77th I was tired and bone-chilled. Slipped into a Rite Aid pharmacy, just long enough to warm and recharge. And out. When I reached 79th, I spotted the bus up ahead idling at the stop. Ran. Caught it. Huffing, puffing, and pleased with myself as I swiped my Metrocard and turned: There he was! Sitting right before my eyes—in the bank of seats closest to the driver, facing the entrance. Face and torso covered by the newsprint tent that was the unfurled New York Times, he, ostensibly, was reading. The one-of-a-kind putrescent-brown-colored ankle-length coat. The old psychic space eater! Taking up three seats though, officially, his bottom occupied only one forcing anyone who wishes to sit there to engage him. Refusing to prolong fate's little joke, I hotfooted it to the middle of the bus, and an instant before the bus pulled out, managed to exit.

Having absorbed the cost of bus fare, I now decided to splurge. Dove straight into a cab. Twelve blocks in no time. Handed the driver a $5 bill, buck tip, and told him to keep the change. Decompressing, I began walking the short distance into the lobby of my building. Glanced down at a medium sized, standing, black mutt. Brought a smile to my face. Looked up at its lolling owner, and smiled at the furry-earmuffed, bright-brown-eyed young woman. Blankly, she looked right through me. I quickly turned away and walked on through the revolving door.

Yes, that's what she said. I was quite certain. "He's not right—in the head." About me, I heard all right, all right. To our mutual neighbor, in the hallway, as I turned the key to open my ground floor apartment door. A woman of about a hundred years, slumped over her walker, said that to another lady of at least eighty.

Why? Because I have not spoken to any of the other tenants in this three floor urban walk-up in the eleven years I've lived here? Or, maybe because they hear me coming or going in the middle of the night? I do nod hello. Well, let them say what they will. I do not want to—ever—have to engage in small talk with any of them.

Inside, I turn the lock shut. Who am I? I'm a man like any other man. More so in some ways, less in others. I drink more coffee but I bed less women. A middle-aged civil servant, I am ordinary-looking and I pay my bills on time. Perfectly fit and unattached. I undress and hit the sack.

In bed, I lie on my back and replay my flirtation with the new waitress in the Rainbow. Suzie. As usual, I ate supper at the Rainbow Diner. Right after she took my order, before I could conjure up a case against her, I introduced myself. Our eyes locked steady. "I'm Suzie," she then declared, breaking the spell. She smiled sweetly. Pretty Suzie, of fair complexion and shoulder-length, straight, light-brown hair, back in a ponytail. The short shiny black skirt she wore wrapped nice on her rounded behind. Discreetly, I continued to feast an eye upon her...When she served my coffee and burger-deluxe (includes fries and a tiny paper cup of coleslaw), I smiled. And ate . . .

Meal devoured, I placed two dollars under the empty cup and headed up to the counter to pay. Despite an electrical current of intestinal anxiety, I forced myself to detour four steps, to Suzie, who was busy serving a table of two. Said, "Good night."

As she whisked by, she affectionately tapped my left elbow with her free hand and replied, "G'night."

Tomorrow, or the day after, I will do it. I'll ask Suzie out. No later. No matter what. Well all right! Now, home for some rest.

After my usual four fitful hours of dreamless sleep I awoke. Shaken and stiff. It was 2:00 AM. I knew I would not be able to fall back asleep for at least an hour. So, I got up. Pissed, dressed, and went out to walk.

It was warm for a late October night and my light sweatshirt felt just right. Walking provided relief. I walked along Center Street, for some ten minutes, passing the gated storefronts and a few other solitary men in drift, when my mellowing mood was badly jarred. Led Zeppelin's over overblown, existential bubblegum rock-anthem "Stairway to Heaven" BOOMED from a passing van SO LOUD my internal organs—almost—burst. To escape, and lessen exposure to passing cars, I spurted ten or so yards to the corner, by the twenty-four hour Shell station, and turned left down a residential street.

Less than a quarter of a block in front of me, on the same side of the sleeping, tree-lined street, I could see the backs of a couple leisurely walking side by side. The trim girl wore white jeans. I'd bet on a pretty girl. Very pretty. Her partner was a medium-sized guy. Short hair and a sweatshirt. From the back, he could be me.

I sped up my pace and closed the gap, but made sure not to get close enough for them to hear my steps. I had a thousand eyes—I had nothing better to do.

Well before the end of the long block, by the driver side of a parked car, they stopped and talked.

I stepped into the dimly lit doorway of a small apartment building, from where I'd be able to continue to spy on them. Suddenly, a woman popped out from behind the other side of the car and joined the guy—in PUMMELING the girl in white jeans. All appeared blurry. The pummel momentum very quickly landed the girl on her back—on the hood of the car. The female half of the assault duo then paused and poked her partner on his shoulder. She pointed across the street. At a laughing man, who was looking back at them and holding up a video camera. He had all of it on tape! Me too? My cowardice would be exposed! Or worse, I'll be indicted as an accomplice! I turned and walked away, briskly. Like an assassin, fleeing the scene of his hit.

It was a quarter of three when I entered my apartment. Collapsing onto the loveseat in my living room. I had purchased the brown leather loveseat this past year. It was very comfortable.

A state employee for close to fifteen years—I process food stamp applications—I decided to spend some savings on new furnishings. Modest, but new. The place was now female-company friendly. I even painted. The walls however remain undecorated.

But the ugly business of tonight has ruined everything. In this very loveseat, I had hoped to sit, with Suzie, and chat intimately. Our fine conversation intermingling with the exquisite sounds of Brahms' intermezzos would scrub the air. Ah, but what will she think of me now? And what will the old bats whisper?

Two hours chewed a deep tunnel of blue doom through my head, before I realized that I was guilty—of nothing. And anyway, if accused, I will deny—deny—deny. Even if I am presented with my own image on video, I will deny that it is me.

When the Saturday morning sun rose I laid down to sleep. I imagined that old bat whispering, "He's not right—in the head," about me, and proceeded to tighten the muscles of my right thigh, in order to change the channel in my head, to sweet thoughts of Suzie—before falling asleep.

Warm, soft hands caressed my stubbled face.

"Those hands feel good," I said.

"They are good," replied Suzie.

Opening my eyes, I knew it was way past noon.

I made a pot of coffee, and remained standing by the kitchen counter as I drank a cup. I figured I'd do some light cleaning around the apartment. But instead, I left the shades drawn over all the windows and went into the living room. Flicked on the TV. And sat in my loveseat.

I kept the sound off, and watched an attractive red-headed girl-next-door type, in a navy-blue jacket, begin to deliver the news. There was a knock on the door to my apartment. When I got there, no one was there. Perhaps that was a cryptic message from the laughing man with the tape! No, I consoled myself, I was simply—just hearing things.

On TV the same woman newscaster seamlessly shifted her expression back and forth from a smile to seriousness. Now and then, she'd slightly tilt her head left, alluringly. Less often, flashing her bare right palm. It was we two. And finally, craning her neck for exclamatory purposes. Why, she could have been reporting on anything, from world hunger to Courtney Love!

In the shower I soaped up heavily. Finished showering. I toweled myself dry and combed my hair. Taking more time than usual to shave, I successfully avoided nicks.

After changing into fresh Fruit of the Looms and getting a refill of coffee, I went into the living room and put on a CD. The songs of early country blues artist—Blind Willie McTell.

*Feel like a broke down engine ain't got no drivin' wheel...*His vocals and guitar strumming, however, rose joyfully above the pained words. Sitting in my loveseat, head bopped to rhythm, gently. *I went down to my prayin' ground and fell on bended knees . . .*

I remained seated, when the music ended. Eyes open or shut, mind's grainy image of Suzie...fell apart. But the shadow of love strengthened my heart.

Locked on my—make a date with Suzie—mission, it was 6:00 PM when I left my apartment for the direct to Rainbow ten minute walk.

The Rainbow was packed but I couldn't wait. Inside, I stood in front by the cashier and scanned the floor for Suzie. Since there was only one dining room—and it was brightly lit—this wasn't difficult.

I needed to see if she was working. In no more than half a minute, I spotted her as she emerged from the back of the room. She had gotten a short haircut!

Balancing a tray of food on her left shoulder and palm, she was coming from the pick-up area of the kitchen. The short haircut looked cute on her. She'd no longer have to wear her hair back while working. From where I stood, Suzie actually looked trimmer than she did yesterday. Different. No matter. She looked mighty good last night and she looks mighty good tonight. Although her station was full, she glanced my way and appeared to notice me. How would it look if I left now, only to come back and sit in her station? Shamefully transparent!

Because I was alone, the owner, an easy going Greek named George, who also served as host, politely motioned me over to the counter.

The layout at the Rainbow was standard. A long counter, where customers dined sitting on swivel stools, ran parallel to four rows of connected family-sized booths. The rows were separated by aisles. The only unusual thing about the entire diner was the very large color portrait of George Washington which hung prominently on the far wall.

Part of the station Suzie worked tonight was in the first aisle. Right behind my seat! All I had to do was turn around. I may not be able to make my move, but I will reinforce our relationship.

Not too bad, except I was hemmed in at the counter. At my left elbow was a pock-marked, pot-bellied, old ashtray that was a man choking a racing form and grumbling about cold coffee and a fixed race. And at my right elbow was a bearish, blond-bearded, young man in a filthy red down-vest. He was reading a book, which he held, eye-level, in his left hand. All the text had been highlighted in orange or green. The book had to do with quantum theory. Couldn't I at least have a polished little lady on one side of me?

I ordered my usual coffee and burger-deluxe from the Mexican counterman. He was all business. Over my left shoulder, I looked upon Suzie, as she worked the tables on the other side of the aisle. I wanted, merely, to make eye-contact and smile hello. She was being coy. I'd have to wait until she was right before me and say hello. I didn't have to wait long.

I was turned fully around, watching her, as she stepped over to wait on the table in front of me. For a moment, we were face to face. And I called her name, "Hi Suzie!" When she did not instantly reply, I repeated, "Hi Suzie!" Again, she did not respond. She was looking right at my face, but seemed not to see me. As though I was no more than a glass window. Mocking eyes of other customers fixed on me, burning a hole into my neck. Got up. And without a word, marched out.

I started walking. Making sure to stay away from where last night's pummeling of the girl in white jeans incident occurred. THAT'S WHAT I GET FOR TRYING! It was another unseasonably mild night.

I don't get it. I don't get it, at all. I could understand—if she turned me down. But, why TOTALLY ignore me? Either I'm crazy or she's crazy. Or, we're both crazy. The hell with the Rainbow. From now on, I eat at home and save money.

I vow to forget tonight. I need to be more calculating and self-centered. Yes, that's the way it must be. The energy of the anger has cleared up my head. I feel more alive. I need to hold on to that.

I passed four check-cashing centers, a Gothic cathedral, and three Blockbuster video superstores.

On air, I walked, tirelessly.

Cut through half-a-dozen schoolyards, across one highway and over another.

Stopped to talk to a homeless man, on a dead-end, dog-litter minefield of a street. And turned, to walk away—when they appeared and blocked my path. They let him run away.

Their leader was a tall, well-built, light-skinned black man, with a shaved head. He wore a full-length black leather coat and stood directly in front of me, about five feet away. Silently, arms crossed. Eyes on me.

He was flanked on each side by a bull-headed, stocky, white midget in a tank-top. The pair cast their flat stares on my kneecaps. Each midget focusing on the kneecap closest in line to his position.

I knew I had to act quickly, because, any moment, the leader would signal for the gang to attack. My plan—blitz the leader. Thereby, scaring off the two sawed-off minotaurs, and making it one on one.

Not many guys in this predicament could pull that off. And I was not one of them.

I readied myself for a runaway charge through the curbside midget into the night, when an eerie sense of clear headedness possessed me...And the fingers of my now raised hands danced a spell on the leader of the ominous threesome. His body dissipated. All that was left of him was his cleanly shaven head, which now rolled like a brown bowling ball, away, off the curb into the gutter.

If that spell worked so thoroughly to obliterate a menacing gang leader, imagine what it would do to you! The midgets did.

It was 9:00 PM when I returned home. A man in charge, I sat in my loveseat and promptly fell into a dreamless sleep.

I awoke almost two hours later, feeling like a wooden board. Needing to walk that off, I took a light jacket from the closet, and headed out.

A street cooling breeze massaged my being. I loosened. Turned up my jacket collar, and contemplated in which direction to walk. The block where the girl in white jeans was pummeled must be avoided. And the way to the Rainbow was now also out. South, was acceptable. Because I always preferred to be within striking distance of the Rainbow, I hadn't walked south in quite a while. Maybe there'd be a new diner. I'd have coffee. There was a bounce to my steps. Yes, I thought, the resourceful heroism that I exhibited against the gang earlier tonight was indeed closest to who I really am.

At the end of the block, I consider stopping, to mambo with a time-expired, shoulder-high parking meter, but for that I feel too self-conscious. Anyhow, I don't know how to mambo. I cross the street.

Under the lurid light of a lamppost, straight ahead about a quarter of a block—arms flail. LEG AFIRE! A lone woman beats her purse wildly against her thigh!

Unhesitatingly, I dash over to aid her, and see, not a fire raging on her leg, but a large red mutt of a dog fastened to her leg blindly humping!

"GET THAT FUCKING THING OFF ME!" She yells at me, from behind the swarming, light-brown curtain of her long, flying hair as she continues to beat the—evidently—sexually aroused dog on his big head with her purse. Which worked him up, even more.

But the son of a bitch didn't know what hit him after I unleashed a vicious running kick into his ribs—he crumbled. There was no fight in him.

A hero, I turned to the ruffled woman I had rescued, who now tossed her hair from her face—

"Suzie...! That waitress last night only looked like—"

"YOU! YOU FUCKING CREEP!" she shrieked, trembling finger damning my face. "YOU PROBABLY SET THIS WHOLE THING UP!"

About NYQ Books™

NYQ Books™ was established in 2009 as an imprint of The New York Quarterly Foundation, Inc. Its mission is to augment the New York Quarterly poetry magazine by providing an additional venue for poets already published in the magazine. A lifelong dream of NYQ's founding editor, William Packard, NYQ Books™ has been made possible by both growing foundation support and new technology that was not available during William Packard's lifetime. We are proud to present these books to you and hope that you will continue to support The New York Quarterly Foundation, Inc. and our poets and that you will enjoy these other titles from NYQ Books™:

Please visit our website for these and other titles:

www.nyqbooks.org

Breinigsville, PA USA
01 September 2009
223366BV00002B/20/P